Who Are the Anglicans?

Profiles and maps of the Anglican Communion With brief descriptions of inter-Anglican agencies and their history

Charles Henry Long, Editor

Prepared for the Lambeth Conference 1988

Forward Movement Publications

©1988. Forward Movement Publications, 412 Sycamore Street, Cincinnati, Ohio, 45202. Printed in U.S.A.

Table of Contents

A Litany for Lambeth

Empowered by the Spirit, and through Jesus Christ, whom we confess as Lord, we give thanks and praise to the Father, calling on him who is the judge of all:

Father, Your Kingdom come

For all the peoples of the world; that they may know you as the God of Peace.

Father, Your Kingdom come

For nations, leaders and governments, that integrity may mark all their dealings.

Father, Your Kingdom come

For all who labour for righteousness, that your presence may give them courage.

Father, Your Kingdom come

For communities torn by dissension and strife that your forgiveness may bring them healing.

Father, Your Kingdom come

For the Church, your household and family, that united in faith and love she may be firm in the confession of her hope.

Father, Your Kingdom come

For the bishops of your church: for all who minister and bear Christ's name that our lives may proclaim your glory.

Father, Your Kingdom come

PREFACE

The information in this book is compiled from many sources and with the help of many people. The editor wishes to acknowledge especially the contribution of Louis Day of Philadelphia who drew the maps, the Rev. Steven Commins of the University of California Los Angeles who developed the format for Provincial Profiles and gathered much preliminary data, and the staff of the Anglican Consultative Council for their research assistance and advice.

Reliable church statistics are notoriously difficult to secure and terms that are used do not always mean the same thing to different people. Does 'number of clergy' include all three orders or only priests? Does 'number of parishes' mean all congregations or only certain legal entities? In the compilation of this book there was not time to clarify such questions or to verify some of the estimates given. The editor believes that the figures given for each Province are reliable as a general guide, but they are not in every case comparable with other Provinces or with reports given to previous Lambeth Conferences.

We have relied primarily on information or statistics supplied by Provincial Secretaries or published yearbooks. We are particularly indebted to Dr. David Barrett and the *World Christian Encyclopedia* (1982) for which he served as general Editor. It contains a wealth of information about the history and the social and religious context of Anglican churches wherever they are found.

The editor apologizes for deficiencies in the maps and profiles of certain extra-provincial dioceses and new dioceses where proper information could not be obtained by press time. He alone is responsible for any gross inaccuracies in the figures given and would be grateful to receive corrected information for use in future publications.

—CHL

1

The Compasrose:
Its Origin and Meaning

The emblem of the Anglican Communion, the Compasrose, was designed by the Rev. Canon Edward N. West, of the Cathedral of St. John the Divine, New York City. The original wooden model of the emblem was six feet in diameter and was made for the second international Anglican Congress in Minneapolis in 1954.

At the center of the circular emblem is the red cross of St. George on a silver shield, a reminder of the origins of the Anglican Communion and a unifying link of the past within the communion today.

Encircling the cross is a band bearing the inscription "The Truth shall make you free" in the original New Testament Greek, the language studied by all scholars within the communion. This quotation, from St. John's Gospel, was also the text of the opening sermon preached at the second Congress, by the then Archbishop of Canterbury, the Most Rev. Geoffrey Francis Fisher.

From the band radiate the points of the compass, the major divisions colored in gold and blue and the minor divisions in green and gold. The compass symbolizes the world-wide spread of the Anglican faith.

Surmounting the shield, at the north, is a mitre, the symbol of the Apostolic Order which is essential to all the churches which constitute the Anglican Communion.

Today the Compasrose is used throughout the Anglican Communion as a symbol of the Anglican family of churches. It is also the logo of the Anglican Consultative Council.

What Is the Anglican Communion?

The Anglican Communion—a term which was coined in 1885—includes an estimated 70 million people in more than 450 dioceses located on all the continents of the world. They include more than 64,000 individual congregations in 164 countries, organized as 28 independent, self-governing, national or regional churches known as Provinces. The member churches of the Anglican Communion represent the world in miniature, a wide variety of races, languages, cultures and political conditions. They are nevertheless one worldwide family, held together by affection for one another, loyalty to common traditions and the continuing practice of consultation and mutual support.

The churches of the Anglican Communion:

• trace their origins to the form and expression of the Christian faith which developed in the Church of England and through its missionary expansion throughout the British Isles and to other lands after the Reformation and in association with other Episcopal or Anglican churches until the present day.

• are in communion with the See of Canterbury (and with one another) freely recognizing the Archbishop of Canterbury as the principal Archbishop and the focus of unity within the Communion.

• uphold and propagate catholic and apostolic faith and order, based on the scriptures and interpreted in the light of Christian tradition, scholarship and reason. This process has found expression in the prayer books and ordinals of the 16th and 17th centuries and in their modern successors.

History

While the Anglican Communion as such is a relatively recent development, its English roots go back to the unknown soldiers and traders who first brought Christianity to England under the Roman Empire. By 341 it had been firmly established in England but the Saxon invasion pushed the young church west and north.

The Celtic churches gradually began the task of trying to convert the invaders and at the same time St. Augustine was sent by Pope Gregory the Great for this purpose. Augustine became the first Archbishop of Canterbury (597-604) converted Ethelbert, the king of Kent, and appointed new bishops for the ancient dioceses of Rochester and London. His personal attempts at reconciliation of the Roman and Celtic churches ended in failure but further negotiations in the 7th century, as at the Synod of Whitby in 664, proved more successful.

The Reformation in England caused no break in the continuity of the office of Archbishop of Canterbury. The English sovereign replaced the Pope as head of the Church of England. Archbishop Thomas Cranmer (1533-1556) accepted the Act of Supremacy in 1534.

The Anglican Communion has developed in two stages. Beginning in the 17th century, Anglicanism was established by colonization in countries such as Australia, Canada, New Zealand, Southern Africa and the eastern part of the present USA. Colonial bishoprics were set up under the authority of Canterbury in many parts of the British Empire; in other parts (e.g. North America) the Bishop of London exercised a distant supervision of local churches. When the American colonies achieved independence a new plan was needed. In 1784, Samuel Seabury of Connecticut was consecrated in Scotland. This was followed by more consecrations of bishops for the USA (and elected in the USA) and by the establishment in 1789 of the first independent daughter church of the Church of England, the Protestant Episcopal Church of the USA. The two churchs were in full communion and had many informal relationships but no formal or legal ties, thus setting a pattern for the Anglican Communion of the future.

The second stage of development was the result of missionary expansion in the 19th and 20th centuries to other countries of Asia, Africa and Latin America and the formation of independent Provinces of the church in what was to become the British Commonwealth. The growth of autonomy in various branches of Anglicanism and the need for consultation led to the first Lambeth Conference in 1867.

Today

The church in England was for many centuries a constituent part of the Western or Latin church, headed by the Bishop of Rome. It has also been for centuries the Church of England "by law established," with particular rights and responsibilities in the political and social life of the nation as a whole. In contrast, most other Anglican Provinces have no memory of being part of the Roman Catholic Church and no experience of the privileges and problems of establishment. Their own histories are relatively brief and they are more likely to be minority churches, sometimes tiny minorities, in societies dominated by other faiths, by other Christian communions or they may find themselves, as in North America, only one of many religious bodies.

It has been said that the Anglican Communion is rapidly outgrowing its Englishness but has not yet established its own identity as a multiracial, multilingual, multicultural family. It has never had a central executive authority or a legislative body able to make decisions for the Communion as a whole nor does there seem to be any great desire to develop such structures. Nevertheless Lambeth 1988 will have to face the question of the inter-relation of Anglican international bodies.

It is aptly named a communion since it comes alive in worship and mutual intercession, in shared experience of community in the body of Christ, in the bonds of affection developed for one another by Anglican leaders at Lambeth Conferences and other meetings and in consultation and encouragement through a variety of instruments for inter-Anglican partnership.

The Lambeth Conference

The Lambeth Conference had its origin in 1865 when, on 20 September, the Provincial Synod of the Church of Canada unanimously agreed to urge the Archbishop of Canterbury and the Convocation of his Province to find a means by which the bishops consecrated within the Church of England and serving overseas could be brought together for a general council to discuss issues facing them in North America, and elsewhere. Part of the background for this request was a serious dispute about the interpretation and authority of the Scriptures which had arisen in Southern Africa between Robert Gray, Archbishop of Cape Town and Bishop Colenso, Bishop of Natal.

Notwithstanding the opposition of a significant number of the bishops in England, Archbishop Longley invited Anglican bishops to their first conference together at Lambeth Palace on 24 September, 1867, and the three following days. Seventy six bishops finally accepted the invitation and the Conference was called to order and met in the chapel of Lambeth Palace. A request to use Westminster Abbey for a service was not granted.

Of the seventy six bishops attending the first Lambeth Conference the distribution was the following: England 18, Ireland 5, Scotland 6, Colonial and missionary bishops 28, United States 19.

It was made clear at the outset that the conference would have no authority of itself as it was not competent to make declarations or lay down definitions on points of doctrine. It did not take any effective action regarding the issues raised by Bishop Colenso but it explored many aspects of possible inter-Anglican cooperation.

In 1878 the second Lambeth Conference was convened by Archbishop Tait and 100 bishops attended. The heavy agenda included "Modern forms of infidelity." It marked another milestone in the growth of the relationship of diverse parts of the Anglican Communion and reinforced the value of the meeting of Anglican bishops to share their common experience.

One hundred and forty five bishops attended the Lambeth Conference of 1888 called by Archbishop Benson. Meeting at Lambeth Palace in the library, its agenda addressed such contemporary issues as intemperance, purity, divorce, care of immigrants and socialism. More important for the ongoing life of the church itself the agenda concerned itself with the issues of ecumenism. In 1886 the General Convention of the Episcopal Church in the United States, meeting in Chicago, had derived a formula which provided a basic framework of recognition of 'authentic' Christian tradition. This formula, known as the Chicago Quadrilateral, was a statement, from the Anglican standpoint, of the essentials for a reunited Christian Church. The four main elements were:

1. The Holy Scriptures of the Old and New Testaments, as 'containing all things necessary to Salvation,' and as being the rule and ultimate standard of Faith.

2. The Apostles' Creed, as the Baptismal symbol; and the Nicene Creed, as the sufficient statement of the Christian Faith.

3. The two Sacraments ordained by Christ himself—Baptism and the Supper of Our Lord—ministered with unfailing use of Christ's words of institution, and of the elements ordained by him.

4. The Historic Episcopate.

The **1888** conference taking this statement, promulgated the first of several successive versions of what has become known as "The Chicago-Lambeth Quadrilateral," a major contribution of the Anglican Communion to the evolving search for unity among the churches.

The **1897** Lambeth Conference was attended by 194 bishops and presided over by Archbishop Frederick Temple. There were two main matters of interest. Firstly, the conference warmly commended the concept of deaconesses; and, secondly, it asked for the establishment of a Consultative Committee which was to be the direct ancestor of the Anglican Consultative Council.

The conference of **1908** with Archbishop Davidson in the chair was attended by 242 bishops and concerned itself with the issues of the ministry of healing, the possible revision of the prayer book and the supply and training of the clergy.

The Lambeth Conference should have convened again in 1918 but this was postponed due to the outbreak of the Great War. Much had changed in the way in which many people understood the world around them when the next conference met in **1920**. This conference, attended by 252 bishops, was dominated by the subject of church unity. The celebrated "Appeal to All Christian People" which was promulgated at the 1920 conference invited other churches to accept episcopacy as the indispensable precondition for their unity with Anglicans. Developing from the consideration of the 1897 conference there was also greater sympathy for a more prominent role for women in the governing and in the ministry of the church. The 1920 conference addressed itself to the issue of contraception and rejected its use outright.

The **1930** conference was presided over by Archbishop Cosmo Lang, 307 bishops in attendance. It proved to be a very crowded occasion in the Lambeth Palace library. The momentum towards church unity in South India found support, encouraging Anglicans in the Indian sub-continent to enter seriously into discussions related to a United Church in India.

Archbishop Geoffrey Fisher presided over two conferences—**1948** attended by 349 bishops and **1958** attended by 310 bishops. By 1948 the Church of South India was an accomplished fact. In 1958 the United Church of North India was welcomed. Nuclear disarmament was an issue in 1958 with the majority being in favor of disarmament and the report on the family was a milestone with its sensitive treatment of the subject of contraception within marriage. The 1958 conference approved the appointment of the first Anglican Executive Officer (Bishop Stephen F. Bayne) thus assisting in the evolution both of the role of the Archbishop of Canterbury and of inter-Anglican structures. This was also the first conference in which wives of the bishops were taken into account in the planning and organization.

The conference of **1968**, under Archbishop Ramsey, was attended by 462 bishops. With this conference it was no longer possible to meet at Lambeth Palace and the conference was thus convened in the Church Assembly Hall at Church House, Westminster. Preparatory papers were offered to members of the conference written by expert consultants and some 35 committees prepared the work for the final report. The issue of the ordination of women came forward and a proposed constitution for the establishment of the Anglican Consultative Council was agreed to.

Another change of venue was to find the **1978** conference meeting residentially in the University of Kent in Canterbury under Archbishop Coggan. Living and worshiping together gave a new community dynamic to the conference. Again, preparatory work was a key element in the deliberations of the conference and an important factor in this was the development of the work and role of the Anglican Consultative Council whose full Standing Committee was present for the conference. Among the important and controversial issues on the agenda of the 1978 conference was the subject of the ordination of women to the priesthood, the training of bishops, human rights, and the evolving inter-Anglican bodies.

Some Important Dates in Anglican History

563	Columba's mission to Iona; Gregory sends Augustine (of Canterbury) to Kent 596
625	Paulinus, Bishop of York
664	Synod of Whitby; Theodore of Tarsus 690, Bede 735
800	Charlemagne revives Roman Empire in the West; Moslems defeated at Tours 732
1054	Final East-West split. Anselm 1109, Aquinas 1274
1384	John Wiclif translates the Bible and advocates reforms; John Hus of Bohemia 1415
1517	Martin Luther's 95 Theses; Zwingli in Zurich 1519; Anabaptists 1524; Calvin in Geneva 1536
1534	Act of Supremacy; English Church independent of Rome under Henry VIII, some reforms
1549	First English Prayer Book and major reforms under Edward VI, Cranmer
1553	Queen Mary returns Church to Rome; persecutions; Cranmer and others burned 1556
1558	Elizabeth reinstitutes reforms; excommunicated by Pope 1570; Puritan controversies
1607	American colonies: Jamestown (Church of England); 1620 Plymouth Pilgrims (Separatist); 1630 Puritans in Massachusetts Bay
1611	Authorized (King James) version of Bible
1649	England under the Commonwealth. Restoration 1660
1662	Act of Uniformity, Book of Common Prayer
1699	Founding of SPCK, Society for the Propagation of Christian Knowledge
1701	Founding of SPG, first Anglican missionary society
1739	Wesleyan Societies started in England. 1784 Methodist Church organized in America
1784	Seabury consecrated in Scotland for American Episcopal Church; organized, 1789
1799	Founding of Church Missionary Society
1867	First Lambeth Conference
1948	World Council of Churches formed, Amsterdam
1954	Anglican Congress, Minneapolis; 1963, Toronto; M.R.I.
1960	Stephen Bayne, first Executive Officer of the Anglican Communion
1971	First meeting Anglican Consultative Council, Limuru, Kenya

The Anglican Consultative Council

Partnership House, 157 Waterloo Road
London SE1 8UT, England
Telephone: 01-620-1110

Origins

An Anglican Consultative Council (ACC) was formed following a resolution of the 1968 Lambeth Conference which discerned the need for more frequent and more representative contact between the churches than was possible through a once-a-decade conference of bishops. The constitution of the Council was accepted by the general synods or conventions of all the member churches of the Anglican Communion. The Council came into being in October 1969 with Bishop John Howe of Scotland as its first Secretary General.

Precursors

Early in the 20th century, Lambeth Conferences arranged for a continuation committee to be appointed, known as the Lambeth Consultation Body, to help the Archbishop of Canterbury deal with any matters he referred to it. The committee was without staff or budget of its own and because of the difficulty and cost of international travel seldom met. Lambeth 1958 tried to remedy the situation by providing for a full-time secretary who would serve both the Lambeth Consultative Body and a new inter-Anglican agency, the Advisory Council on Missionary Strategy. This led to the appointment of Stephen Bayne, Bishop of Olympia, USA to serve as the first Executive Officer of the Anglican Communion (1960-64) with offices in London.

Through tireless travel, speaking and writing, Bishop Bayne was able to strengthen communications among the Provinces and to develop a new vision of Anglicanism in the modern world. This came to a vivid expression in the Anglican Congress held in Toronto in 1963.

Bishop Bayne was succeeded by Ralph Dean, Bishop of Cariboo, Canada (1964-69) and then by Bishop John Howe of Scotland (1969-82). With the formation of the ACC Bishop Howe's title was changed to Secretary General. The Reverend Canon Samuel VanCulin, USA, became Secretary General in 1983.

The Role of the ACC

At its inception the Council was given eight terms of reference and its responsibilities include:

- Sharing information and co-ordinating common action
- Developing agreed policies and initiatives for world mission
- Developing and maintaining ecumenical relations
- Promoting research and inquiry
- Creating networks of key persons involved with social concerns
- Advising member churches on constitutional matters

The Council does not have legislative powers. Each self governing church draws on advice and information from the ACC and makes decisions in the light of local needs and culture.

The core budget of ACC is supported by all member churches of the Anglican Communion according to their membership and means.

Membership

Each member church of the Anglican Communion, according to size, is represented by up to three members—one bishop, a member of the clergy, and a lay person. The Council has powers to co-opt up to six members. Two of these are women and two are young persons. The united churches of South India, North India, and Pakistan are full members. Membership currently totals 61.

Meetings

The ACC meets every two or three years (a Standing Committee meets annually) and its present policy is to meet in different parts of the world. There have been 7 meetings of the Council, in Limuru, Kenya (1971); Dublin, Republic of Ireland (1973); Trinidad (1976); London, Ontario, Canada (1979); Newcastle-upon-Tyne, England (1981); Badagry, Nigeria (1984); Singapore (1987).

Some of its chief activities are as follows:

Partners in Mission

The Anglican Congress in Toronto, 1963, said that the resources of each church for mission need to be shared. The Congress coined the term MRI—Mutual Responsibility and Inter-Dependence in the Body of Christ. The second meeting of the ACC at Dublin sought to develop this further through Partnership in Mission. As a result, from time to time member churches invite other churches to be their partners in mission. They call a consultation attended by representatives of their partner churches. At the consultation they clarify their thinking about their mission task and identify priorities. Partnership in Mission is based on the principle that every church can be both a giver and a receiver to the enrichment of the whole mission of the church. Consultations often result in new insights as problems are shared. They also help the churches of the Anglican Communion to share their resources in the most effective way.

Inter-Church Conversations

The Anglican Communion has important continuing dialogues with the Roman Catholic, Orthodox and Lutheran churches. The ACC is responsible for this work on behalf of Anglicans. It has been set the task of co-ordinating the response of member churches of the Anglican Communion to recently completed ecumenical dialogues: Anglican-Roman Catholic, Anglican-Orthodox, Anglican-Lutheran and Anglican-Reformed, and Anglican-Oriental Orthodox. It is also encouraging Anglican churches to study and respond to the document, *Baptism, Eucharist and Ministry,* a product of many years of work involving all major Christian traditions, through the Faith and Order Commission of the World Council of Churches.

Inter-Anglican Theological and Doctrinal Commission

This commission, consisting of fifteen members, clerical and lay, from twelve churches, met for the first time in 1981. Its first report, *For the Sake of the Kingdom,* has been prepared for the Lambeth Conference of 1988. It is a study of the relationship between the church and the Kingdom of God and of the impact of different cultures on theology.

The Anglican Centre in Rome

This Centre was set up in 1966 following the historic visit of Archbishop Michael Ramsey to meet Pope Paul VI. It aims to help Roman Catholic Church leaders and seminarians to develop a better understanding of Anglicanism. It serves as a base for ecumenical contact and maintains a unique resource library on Anglicanism. It provides the Anglican Communion with a listening post in Rome. Through seminars it helps Anglicans to a better understanding of the Roman Catholic Church.

Networks

The ACC encourages and facilitates the work of a number of informal, international networks, composed of provincial specialists in Ecumenical Relations, Peace and Justice issues, Family questions, Mission, Development, Communications, Publishing and Youth Work. They share information and increase collaboration in their various fields of specialization and are often called upon to give advice or undertake research on behalf of the Anglican Communion. The networks are funded by the participants themselves and by grants outside the regular budget of the ACC. Several of the networks have prepared study books for the agenda of the 1988 Lambeth Conference.

Primates and Provinces

Primates meet together every two or three years and represent another important link of partnership in the period between Lambeth Conferences. In their own countries Primates are titled variously as Archbishop, Presiding Bishop, Primus or Metropolitan and by similar terms in other languages. Each is the head of an independent branch or Province of the Anglican Communion. It has been helpful to consult regularly about responsibilities peculiar to their office and about matters of concern to the whole Communion. Primates Meetings have taken place in Ely, England, 1979; Washington, USA, 1981; Limuru, Kenya, 1983 and Toronto, Canada, 1986.

It is sometimes confusing to learn that the dioceses of larger Provinces, such as Canada, Australia and the USA often are organized regionally with internal 'Provinces,' each of which is also under the leadership of an 'archbishop' or, in the USA, a 'president.'

There are occasional inter-provincial Anglican meetings, not always restricted to bishops, in larger geographical regions, such as Africa, Southeast Asia or Latin America. Such regional bodies may either bring together existing Provinces for common planning or represent an interim stage in the formation of new Provinces.

The Church of Burundi, Rwanda, and Zaïre

8

ZAÏRE

1

3

7

RWANDA

4

5

BURUNDI

6

2

1. BOGA-ZAÏRE
   • Bunia
2. BUJUMBURA
   • Bujumbura
3. BUKAVU
   • Bukavu
4. BUTARE
   • Butare
5. BUYE
   • Buye
6. GITEGA
   • Gitega
7. KIGALI
   • Kigali
8. KISANGANI
   • Kisangani

LEGEND

— — — Nation
———— Diocese
● See City

12

The Church of the Province of Burundi, Rwanda and Zaire
La Province du Burundi, Rwanda et Zaire

Countries: Burundi, Rwanda, Zaire
Geographical area: 2,399,172 square kilometers
Population: 35,741,310
Number of Anglicans: 699,970 (2%)
Dioceses: 10 (Boga-Zaire, Bujumbura, Bukavu, Butare, Buye, Gitega, Kigali, Kisangani, Shaba, Shyira)
Number of Christians: 78% of population
        Roman Catholic (53%), Protestant (25%)
Other faiths: Traditional religions (21%), Muslim (1%)

Parishes: 340
Number of clergy: 440
Theological Colleges 3, Bible colleges 15

Brief history: This church was formed as a result of the division of the former Province of Uganda, Rwandi, Burundi and Boga-Zaire in 1980. The first archbishop was Bezaleri Ndahura. The three countries making up the Province are French-speaking. All were formerly ruled by Belgium and the majority of the citizens are Roman Catholic. Anglican work in Rwanda was founded by CMS medical missionaries from Uganda in 1924. A Ugandan evangelist, Apolo Kivebulayo, at the turn of the century crossed snow capped mountains to preach to the people of the Ituri rain forests in Boga-Zaire. The Province is governed by a Synod which meets every four years and by a Standing Committee and House of Bishops which meet twice yearly.

Archbishop: Samuel Sindamuka
Provincial office: B.P. 1300, Bujumbura, Burundi

Note: Diocesan boundaries and the locations of see cities were not available at press time.

The Church of Uganda

8. LANGO
   • Lira
9. MADI and WEST NILE
   • Arua
10. MBALE
    • Mbale
11. MITYANA
    • Mityana
12. MUKONO
    • Mukono
13. NAMIREMBE
    • Kampala
14. NORTH KIGEZI
    • Rukungiri
15. NORTHERN UGANDA
    • Gulu
16. RUWENZORI
    • Fort Portal
17. SOROTI
    • Soroti
18. SOUTH RUWENZORI
    • Kasese
19. WEST ANKOLE
    • Bushenyi
20. WEST BUGANDA
    • Masaka

1. BUKEDI
   • Tororo
2. BUNYORO-KITARA
   • Hoima
3. BUSOGA
   • Jinja
4. EAST ANKOLE
   • Mbarara
5. KAMPALA
   • Kampala
6. KARAMOJA
   • Moroto
7. KIGEZI
   • Kabale

LEGEND

━━━━ ━ ━ ━ Nation
━━━━━━━ Diocese
● See City

The Church of Uganda

Geographical area: 91,134 square miles
Population: 15,500,000
Number of Anglicans: 2,200,000 (25%)
Dioceses: 20 (Bukedi, Bunyoro-Kitara, Busoga, East Ankole, Kampala, Karamo-
ja, Kigezi, Lango, Madi, Mbale, Mityana, Mukono, Namirembe, North
Kigezi, Northern Uganda, Ruwenzori, Soroti, South Ruwenzori, West
Ankole, West Buganda)
Number of Christians: 8,000,000
Roman Catholics, 30% of the population
Other faiths: Traditional religions (13%), Muslim (7%)

Parishes: 6,536
Number of clergy: 800 estimated
Theological Colleges: Bishop Tucker Theological College, Mukono, and 8 others.

Brief history: Missionary work was begun in 1877 by the CMS, responding to
the explorer Stanley's call for missionaries after his visit to the court of Kabaka
Mutesa in 1875. The church grew rapidly, largely through the evangelization
of Africans by other Africans, especially during the East Africa Revival; this
began in 1927 and continues to be an influence today. The first Ugandan clergy
were ordained in 1893 and the church became an independent Province in 1961.
From the first the church has produced its share of martyrs as well as evan-
gelists and has suffered much in times of civil strife. The first bishop, James
Hannington, and his companions were murdered in 1886. Archbishop Janani
Luwum was killed by the tyrant Idi Amin in 1977.

Archbishop: Yona Okoth
Provincial office: P.O. Box 14123, Kampala, Uganda

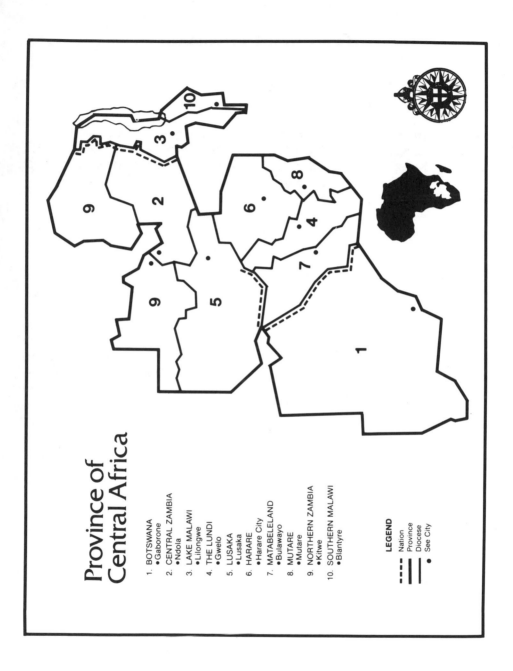

Province of
Central Africa

1. BOTSWANA
    ● Gaborone
2. CENTRAL ZAMBIA
    ● Ndola
3. LAKE MALAWI
    ● Lilongwe
4. THE LUNDI
    ● Gwelo
5. LUSAKA
    ● Lusaka
6. HARARE
    ● Harare City
7. MATABELELAND
    ● Bulawayo
8. MUTARE
    ● Mutare
9. NORTHERN ZAMBIA
    ● Kitwe
10. SOUTHERN MALAWI
    ● Blantyre

LEGEND
- - - - Nation
———— Province
———— Diocese
● See City

Church of the Province of Central Africa

Countries: Botswana, Zambia, Malawi, Zimbabwe
Geographical area: 705,970 square miles
Population: 21,869,117
Number of Anglicans: 600,000
Dioceses: 10 (Botswana, Central Zambia, Harare, Lake Malawi, The Lundi, Lusaka, Manicaland, Matabeleland, Northern Zambia, Southern Malawi)
Number of Christians: 8,165,000
    Roman Catholic (15%), Protestant (15%), African churches (6%)
Other faiths: traditional religions (30%)

Parishes: about 180
Number of clergy: 372

Brief history: The Province was founded in 1955 with the union of the dioceses of Northern Rhodesia (now Zambia), Nyasaland (now Malawi) Mashonaland and Matabeleland (now Zimbabwe). Matabeleland included part of northern Botswana, while the southern part formed part of the diocese of Kimberley and Kuruman.

The dioceses of northern Rhodesia and Nyasaland were under the jurisdiction of the Archbishop of Canterbury and Mashonaland and Matabeleland were under the Archbishop of Capetown. The constitution of the Province is similar to that of other Provinces in Africa.

Archbishop: Khotso Makhulu
Provincial office: P.O. Box 769, Gaborone, Botswana

Province of the Indian Ocean

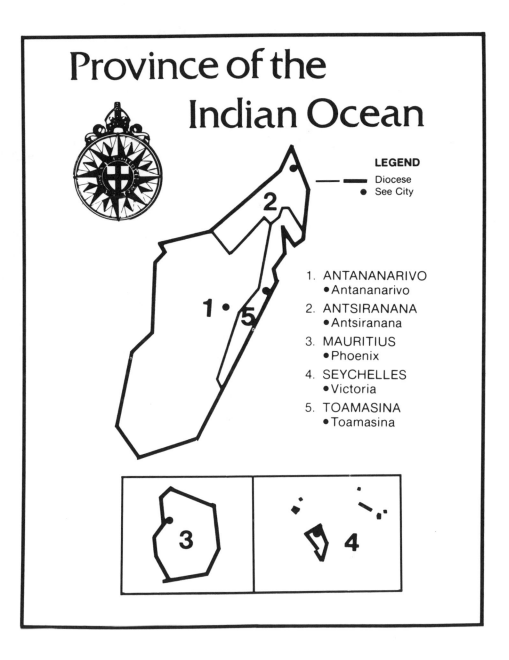

LEGEND
— Diocese
• See City

1. ANTANANARIVO
   • Antananarivo
2. ANTSIRANANA
   • Antsiranana
3. MAURITIUS
   • Phoenix
4. SEYCHELLES
   • Victoria
5. TOAMASINA
   • Toamasina

Church of the Province of the Indian Ocean

Countries: Madagascar, Mauritius, Seychelles
Geographical area: 230,223 square miles
Population: 9,767,000
Number of Anglicans: 83,000
Dioceses: 5 (Antananarivo, Antsiranana, Mauritius, Seychelles Toamasina)
Number of Christians: 5,082,000
           Roman Catholic (30%), Lutheran (6%)
Other faiths: traditional (20%), Hindu (1%), Muslim (3%)

Parishes: 95
Number of clergy: 90
Theological colleges: St. Paul's, Madagascar and St. Philip's, Seychelles

Brief history: The Province of the Indian Ocean was founded in 1973. Prior to that the Seychelles and Mauritius formed one bishopric. Madagascar also had one bishop. The Anglican mission was first established in Mauritius in 1810 after the British captured the island from the French. From Mauritius, missionaries were sent out to the three islands. The Province is governed by a provincial synod which meets every four years. Between sessions a Standing Committee of Synod runs the diocese. The Archbishop is elected for a term of five years which is renewable.

Archbishop: French Chang Him
Provincial office: P.O. Box 44, Mahe, Seychelles
Provincial newspaper or magazine: *Newsletter of the Province of Indian Ocean Support Association*, Editor: Mrs. M. Woodward, Vic., 56 High Street, Brackley, Northants NN13 5DS, England; *Syechelles Diocesan Magazine* (quarterly) and *The Anglican Herald of Mauritius* (a bi-monthly newspaper).

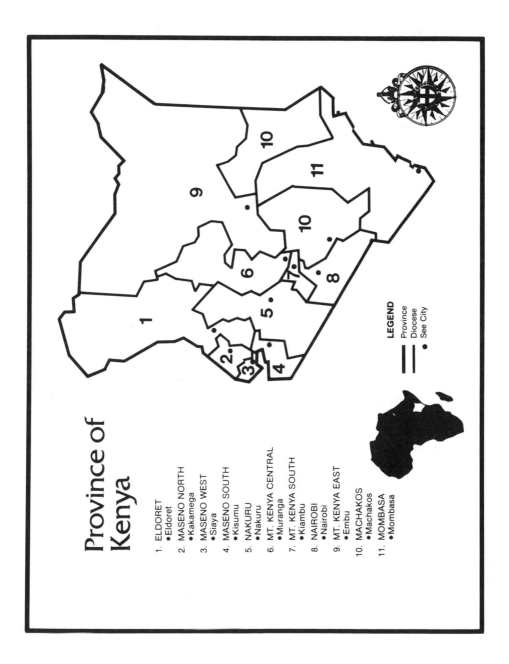

Province of Kenya

1. ELDORET
   • Eldoret
2. MASENO NORTH
   • Kakamega
3. MASENO WEST
   • Siaya
4. MASENO SOUTH
   • Kisumu
5. NAKURU
   • Nakuru
6. MT. KENYA CENTRAL
   • Muranga
7. MT. KENYA SOUTH
   • Kiambu
8. NAIROBI
   • Nairobi
9. MT. KENYA EAST
   • Embu
10. MACHAKOS
    • Machakos
11. MOMBASA
    • Mombasa

LEGEND
— Province
║ Diocese
• See City

Church of the Province of Kenya
Kanisa la Jimbo la Kenya

Geographical Area: 564,162 square miles
Population: estimated 22,000,000
Number Anglicans: estimated 1,300,000
Dioceses: 12 (Eldoret, Machakos, Maseno North, Maseno South, Maseno West,
       Mombasa, Mount Kenya Central, Mount Kenya East, Mount Kenya
       South, Nairobi, Nakuru, Nambale)
Number of Christians: 16,000,000
       Roman Catholic (26%), Protestant (19%), African churches (17%)
Other faiths: traditional (19%), Muslim (6%)
Founding date for Province: 1970

Parishes: 453
Number of clergy: 500
Theological colleges: St. Paul's United Theological Seminary,
       Limuru; 7 Bible colleges

Brief History: Anglican work began in 1844 with the arrival of the first CMS missionary at Mombasa. Rapid growth began later in the 19th century, with the first African ordinations in 1885 and a mass movement of conversions starting in 1910. The Diocese of Mombasa was established in 1927. The first two Kenyan bishops were consecrated in 1955. Besides CMS, the Bible Churchman's Missionary Society played an important role. The church became part of the new Province of East Africa established in 1960. In 1970 the Province was divided into separate Provinces of Kenya and Tanzania.

Archbishop: Manasses Kuria
Provincial office: P.O. Box 40502, Nairobi, Kenya

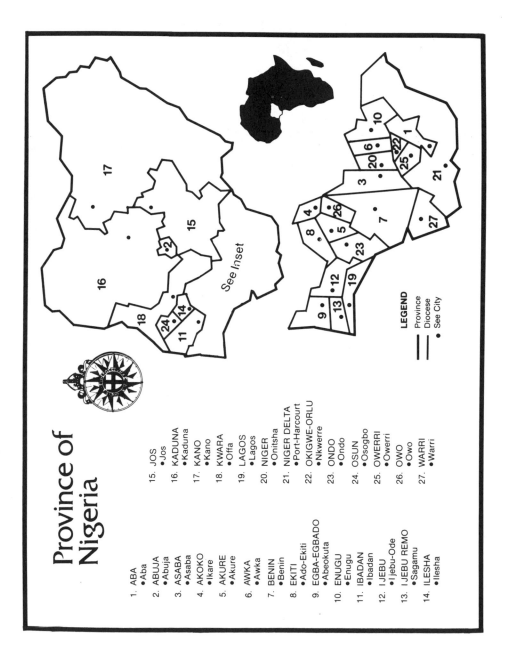

Province of Nigeria

1. ABA
   • Aba
2. ABUJA
   • Abuja
3. ASABA
   • Asaba
4. AKOKO
   • Ikare
5. AKURE
   • Akure
6. AWKA
   • Awka
7. BENIN
   • Benin
8. EKITI
   • Ado-Ekiti
9. EGBA-EGBADO
   • Abeokuta
10. ENUGU
    • Enugu
11. IBADAN
    • Ibadan
12. IJEBU
    • Ijebu-Ode
13. IJEBU REMO
    • Sagamu
14. ILESHA
    • Ilesha
15. JOS
    • Jos
16. KADUNA
    • Kaduna
17. KANO
    • Kano
18. KWARA
    • Offa
19. LAGOS
    • Lagos
20. NIGER
    • Onitsha
21. NIGER DELTA
    • Port-Harcourt
22. OKIGWE-ORLU
    • Nkwerre
23. ONDO
    • Ondo
24. OSUN
    • Osogbo
25. OWERRI
    • Owerri
26. OWO
    • Owo
27. WARRI
    • Warri

LEGEND
— Province
— Diocese
• See City

Church in the Province of Nigeria

Geographical area: 923,768 square miles
Population: 97,000,000
Number of Anglicans: 3,900,000
Dioceses: 26 (Aba, Akoko, Akure, Asaba, Awka, Benin, Egba-Egbado, Ekiti,
Enugu, Ibadan, Ijebu, Ijebu-Remo, Ilesa, Jos, Kaduna, Kano, Kawara,
Lagos, The Niger, The Niger Delta, Okigwe-Orlu, Ondo, Osun,
Owerri, Owo, Warri)
Number of Christians: 32,000,000
Roman Catholic 12.1%, Protestant 15.2%, African churches 10.6%
Other faiths: Muslim 45%, traditional religions 5.6%

Parishes: 3,680
Number of clergy:

Brief history: The first Anglicans in what is now Nigeria were freed slaves from
Sierra Leone. In the 1840s the CMS followed and soon established extensive
educational and evangelistic work. The first African bishop was consecrated
in 1864. Anglicans are now found in every part of the country and are the largest Christian body after the Roman Catholics. The Province was established
in 1979, by division from the Province of West Africa (1951).

Archbishop:
Provincial office: Church House, 29 Marina, P.O. Box 78, Lagos, Nigeria
Provincial magazine: *Magazine of the Church of Nigeria*

Church of the Province of Southern Africa

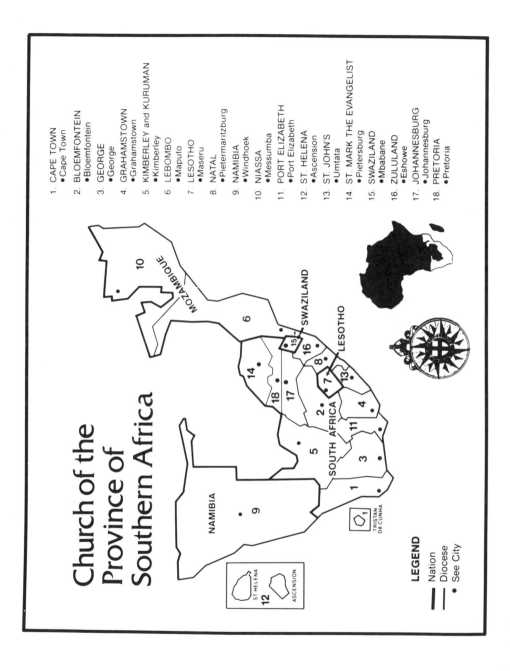

1. CAPE TOWN
   • Cape Town
2. BLOEMFONTEIN
   • Bloemfontein
3. GEORGE
   • George
4. GRAHAMSTOWN
   • Grahamstown
5. KIMBERLEY and KURUMAN
   • Kimberley
6. LEBOMBO
   • Maputo
7. LESOTHO
   • Maseru
8. NATAL
   • Pietermaritzburg
9. NAMIBIA
   • Windhoek
10. NIASSA
    • Messumba
11. PORT ELIZABETH
    • Port Elizabeth
12. ST. HELENA
    • Ascension
13. ST. JOHN'S
    • Umtata
14. ST. MARK THE EVANGELIST
    • Pietersburg
15. SWAZILAND
    • Mbabane
16. ZULULAND
    • Eshowe
17. JOHANNESBURG
    • Johannesburg
18. PRETORIA
    • Pretoria

MOZAMBIQUE

SWAZILAND

LESOTHO

SOUTH AFRICA

NAMIBIA

ST HELENA

ASCENSION

TRISTAN DA CUNHA

LEGEND

| Nation
--- Diocese
• See City

24

Church of the Province of Southern Africa

Countries: South Africa, Namibia, Mozambique, Lesotho, Swaziland, Island
    of St. Helena, Ascension Island, Tristan da Cunha
Geographical area: 2,874,000 square miles
Population: 50,700,000
Number of Anglicans: 2,400,000
Dioceses: 18 (Bloemfontein, Cape Town, George, Grahamstown, Johannesburg,
    Kimberley and Kuruman, Lebombo, Lesotho, Namibia, Natal, Nias-
    sa, Port Elizabeth, Pretoria, Saint Helena, Saint John's, Saint Mark
    the Evangelist, Swaziland, Zululand)
Number of Christians: 28,000,000
    Roman Catholic (9.2%), Protestant (38.2%), African churches (19.9%)
    (for South Africa only)
Other faiths: (for South Africa only) Hindu (1.7%), Muslim 1.1%), traditional
    religions.

Parishes: 770
Number of clergy: 1,200
Seminaries/theological colleges: 4

Brief history: The Province is the oldest in Africa and formerly included parts
of the Province of Central Africa. British Anglicans met regularly for worship
in Cape Town after 1806. The first SPG missionary arrived in 1821. Major growth
began after the establishment of the first diocese, Cape Town, in 1847 and the
appointment of the first bishop. In the same year that the Province was formed,
in 1870, a dissident evangelical group separated to form another church known
as the Church of England in South Africa. The work of the Province was ex-
tended to Lesotho in 1875, to Mozambique in 1893, and in the 20th century to
Namibia and Swaziland. Although Anglicanism is naturally strong among the
descendants of British colonists and other English-speaking people, 75% of the
church's membership is black. Many of its leaders, white and black, have been
strong opponents of apartheid.

Archbishop: Desmond Tutu
Provincial office: Bishopscourt, Claremont, CP 7700, South Africa
Provincial newspaper: *SEEK*

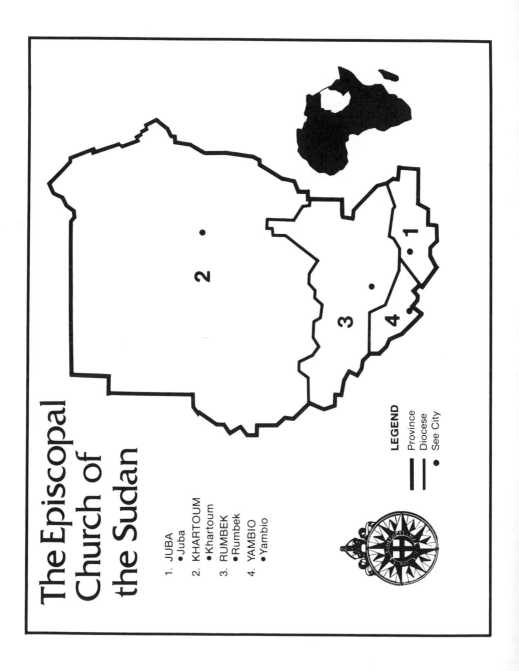

The Episcopal Church of the Sudan

1. JUBA
   • Juba
2. KHARTOUM
   • Khartoum
3. RUMBEK
   • Rumbek
4. YAMBIO
   • Yambio

LEGEND
— Province
= Diocese
• See City

Episcopal Church of the Sudan

Geographical area: 2,505,813 square miles
Population: 27,000,000
Number of Anglicans: estimates vary from 390,000 to 2,500,000
Dioceses: 4 at present (Juba, Khartoum, Rumbek, Yambio)
       7 more proposed (Bor, Kaduguli, Kajokaji, Maridi, Mundri, Wau, Yei)
Number of Christians: estimates vary from 2 to 6 million
       Largest denominations: Roman Catholic and Anglican
Other faiths: Muslim (70%), traditional religions (10%)

Parishes: 275
Number of clergy: 400

Brief history: Although the CMS began work in Omdurman in 1899, in an overwhelmingly Muslim population, Christianity spread more rapidly among black Africans of the southern region. Until 1974 the Sudan was a single diocese under the Archbishop in Jerusalem. In 1974 it was divided into 4 dioceses, each under a Sudanese bishop, and became an independent Province. The church has suffered much in the last generation from almost continual civil and religious strife between north and south and from a constant flow of refugees in and out of the country.

Archbishop: Benjamin W. Yugusuk
Provincial secretary: The Rev. John L. Kanyikwa, c/o ACROSS, P.O. Box 44838, Nairobi, Kenya
Provincial newspaper: *Newsletter of the Episcopal Church of the Sudan*, P.O. Box 110, Juba, Dem. Rep. of the Sudan

Province of Tanzania

1. CENTRAL TANGANYIKA
   • Dodoma
2. DAR ES SALAAM
   • Dar es Salaam
3. KAGERA
   • Murgwanza
4. MARA
   • Musoma
5. MASASI
   • Masasi
6. MOROGORO
   • Morogoro
7. MOUNT KILIMANJARO
   • Arusha
8. RUVUMA
   • Songea
9. SOUTH WEST TANGANYIKA
   • Njombe
10. VICTORIA NYANZA
    • Mwanza
11. WESTERN TANGANYIKA
    • Kasulu
12. ZANZIBAR AND TANGA
    • Korogwe

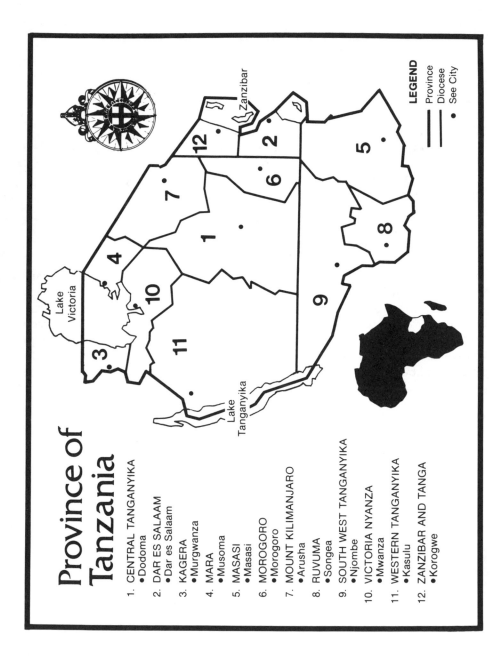

Church of the Province of Tanzania
Kanisa la Jimbo la Tanzania

Geographical area: 945,087 square kilometers
Population: 23,400,000
Number of Anglicans: 1,000,000
Dioceses: 12 (Central Tanganyika, Dar-es-Salaam, Kagera, Mara, Masasi, Morogoro, Mt. Kilimanjaro, Ruvuma, South West Tanganyika, Victoria Nyanza, Western Tanganyika, Zanzibar and Tanga.)
Number of Christians: 8,000,000
        Roman Catholic (21%), Protestant (9%)
Other faiths: Muslim 32%, Hindu .3%

Parishes: 450
Number of clergy: 600
Theological colleges: St. Philip's College, Kongwa and St. Mark's College, Dar es Salaam

Brief history: The Province was founded in 1970 from the former Church of the Province of East Africa with nine dioceses. There are two traditions of Anglicanism, those brought by the former Universities Mission to Central Africa and by the CMS. UMCA began work in 1863, in Zanzibar. CMS work spread from what is now Kenya, beginning in 1886. The Province is governed by the Provincial Synod which meets every three years.

Archbishop: John A. Ramadhani
Provincial office: P.O. Box 899, Dodoma, Tanzania
Provincial newspaper or magazine: *Sauti Ya Jimbo*

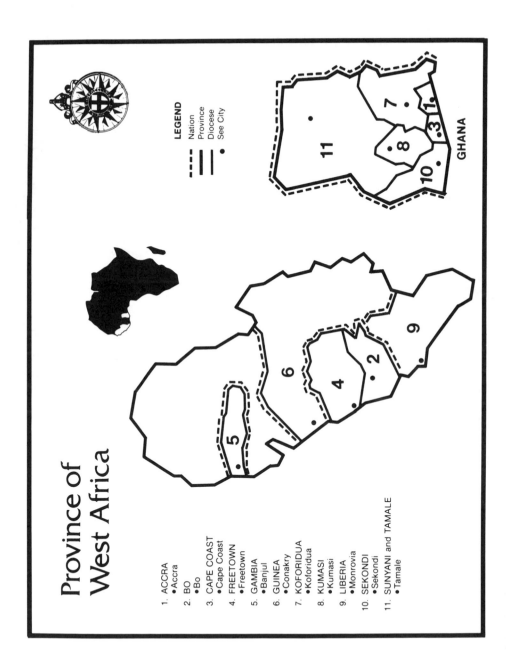

Province of
West Africa

1. ACCRA
   • Accra
2. BO
   • Bo
3. CAPE COAST
   • Cape Coast
4. FREETOWN
   • Freetown
5. GAMBIA
   • Banjul
6. GUINEA
   • Conakry
7. KOFORIDUA
   • Koforidua
8. KUMASI
   • Kumasi
9. LIBERIA
   • Monrovia
10. SEKONDI
    • Sekondi
11. SUNYANI and TAMALE
    • Tamale

LEGEND
Nation
Province
Diocese
• See City

GHANA

30

The Church of the Province of West Africa

Countries: Ghana, The Gambia, Guinea, Liberia, Sierra Leone
Geographical area:
>   seven dioceses, 154,353 square miles
>   four dioceses, 522,519 square miles

Population: 34,844,108
Number of Anglicans: 132,273
Dioceses: 11 (Accra, Bo, Cape Coast, Freetown, The Gambia, Guinea, Koforidua, Kumasi, Liberia, Sekondi, Sunyani and Tamale)
Number of Christians: 3,840,000
>   Roman Catholic (9%), African churches (7%), Protestant (11%)

Other faiths: Muslim (22%), traditional religions (23%)

Parishes: 143
Number of clergy: 291
Theological colleges: Ghana: Trinity College and St. Nicholas Theological College; Liberia: Cuttington University College; Sierra Leone: Theological College, Freetown

Brief history: The Province was founded in 1951, and at that time included the present Province of Nigeria (established 1979). Anglicans were found in Ghana as early as 1752. Work began in other countries of the Province early in the 19th century with the help of SPG and, in Liberia, the Episcopal Church USA. Church growth has been slow to reach beyond the coastal areas of these countries and Christians remain a minority of the total population.

Archbishop: George D. Browne
Provincial office: P.O. Box 8, Accra, Ghana

LEGEND

———	Diocese
— — —	Nation
●	See City

Igreja Episcopal do Brasil

6. CENTRAL
   ● Rio de Janeiro
7. NORTHERN
   ● Recife
8. SOUTHERN
   ● Porto Alegre
9. SOUTH CENTRAL
   ● Sao Paulo
10. SOUTHWESTERN
    ● Santa Maria
11. BRASÍLIA
    ● Brasília

Falkland Islands
(See of Canterbury)

Iglesia Anglicana del Cono Sur de America

1. ARGENTINA and
   URUGUAY
   ● Buenos Aires
2. CHILE
   ● Santiago

3. NORTHERN ARGENTINA
   ● Salta
4. PARAGUAY
   ● Asurcion
5. PERU with BOLIVIA
   ● Lima

The Church of Brazil
Igreja Episcopal do Brasil

Geographical area: 8,511,965 square kilometers
Population: 141,302,000 (1987)
Number of Anglicans: 65,000 (1986)
Dioceses: 6 (Brasilia, Central, Northern, Southern, South Central, Southwestern
        Brazil)
Number of Christians: 113,746,959 (1980)
        Roman Catholic, (80%), Pentecostal, (10%)
Other faiths: Spiritism, (5%), (Afro-brasilian cults)

Parishes: 67
Number of clergy: 108
Theological college: 1

Brief history: Christianity came to Brazil in the 16th century with the Portuguese
conquest. There were Anglican chaplaincies to expatriates after 1810; separa-
tion of Church and State in 1889 allowed non-Roman Catholic missions and
Anglican work was begun by two missionaries from the USA among Brazilians
in two southern states, leading to the establishment of Southern Brazil as a
missionary district of the American church in 1907. The Episcopal Church of
Brazil became an autonomous Province in 1965, but counts its "real birthday"
as June 1, 1980 when it accepted full responsibility for self support. The Province
is governed by a Provincial Synod, of two Houses, which meets every two years.

Presiding Bishop: Olavo V. Luiz
Provincial Office: Caixa Postal 11510, P. Alegre, RS 90641, Brasil
Provincial Newspaper: *Estandarte Cristao*

The Church of the Southern Cone of America
Iglesia Anglicana del Cono Sud de las Americas

Countries: Argentina, Bolivia, Chile, Paraguay, Peru, Uruguay
Geographical area: 2,440,000 square miles
Population: 82,000,000
Number of Anglicans: 27,000
Dioceses: 5 (Argentina and Uruguay; Chile; Northern Argentina; Paraguay;
　　　Peru with Bolivia)
Number of Christians: 71,000,000
　　　Roman Catholic (76%), Protestant (2%)
Other faiths: Jews (1%)
Founding date of province: April 30, 1983

Parishes: 265
Number of clergy: 121 plus 100 missionaries
Theological colleges: Instituto Superior Evangelico de Estudios Theologicos
　　　(ISEDET), Buenos Aires, (ecumenical); Comision de Educacion The-
　　　ologica, Salta; United Theological Seminary, La Molina, Lima, Peru.
　　　Many of the clergy are trained through a theological training by ex-
　　　tension program which is based in Chile.

Brief history: Anglicanism grew from two separate developments. The first was
from the British immigrants who came to South America for commercial reasons and brought their church and priests to minister to the expatriate communities. The second development was from direct missionary endeavors
started by Captain Allen Gardiner amongst the Indians; his work was continued
by the South American Missionary Society from the 1880s.

Presiding Bishop: David Leake, Casilla 187, 4400, Salta, Argentina
Provincial Secretary: The Rev. Juan Zamora, Casilla 561, Vinadel Mar, Chile

The Episcopal Church (USA)

Profile does not include related overseas dioceses.
Geographical area: 3,615,122 square miles
Population: 225,000,000
Number of Anglicans/Episcopalians: 2,504,000
Dioceses: 98, plus 20 overseas jurisdictions, grouped into 9 internal provinces
Province 1: Connecticut, Maine, Massachusetts, New Hampshire, Rhode Island, Vermont, Western Massachusetts. *Province 2:* Albany, Central New York, Convocation of American Churches in Europe, Haiti, Long Island, New Jersey, New York, Newark, Rochester, the Virgin Islands, Western New York. *Province 3:* Bethlehem, Central Pennsylvania, Delaware, Easton, Maryland, Northwestern Pennsylvania, Pennsylvania, Pittsburgh, Southern Virginia, Southwestern Virginia, Virginia, Washington, D.C., West Virginia. *Province 4:* Alabama, Atlanta, Central Florida, Central Gulf Coast, East Carolina, East Tennessee, Florida, Georgia, Kentucky, Lexington, Louisiana, Mississippi, North Carolina, South Carolina, Southeast Florida, Southwest Florida, Tennessee, Upper South Carolina, West Tennessee, Western North Carolina. *Province 5:* Chicago, Eau Claire, Fond du Lac, Indianapolis, Michigan, Milwaukee, Missouri, Northern Indiana, Northern Michigan, Ohio, Quincy, Southern Ohio, Springfield, Western Michigan. *Province 6:* Colorado, Iowa, Minnesota, Montana, Nebraska, North Dakota, South Dakota, Wyoming. *Province 7:* Arkansas, Dallas, Fort Worth, Kansas, Northwest Texas, Oklahoma, Rio Grande, Texas, West Missouri, West Texas, Western Kansas, Western Louisiana. *Province 8:* Alaska, Arizona, California, Central Philippines, Eastern Oregon, El Camino Real, Hawaii, Idaho, Los Angeles, Navajoland, Nevada, Northern California, Northern Luzon, Northern Philippines, Olympia, Oregon, San Joaquin, San Diego, Southern Philippines, Spokane, Taiwan, Utah. *Province 9:* Central and South Mexico, Colombia, Dominican Republic, Ecuador, El Salvador, Guatemala, Honduras, Littoral, Nicaragua, Northern Mexico, Panama, Western Mexico.
Number of Christians: est. 197,344,000
Roman Catholic (30%), Protestants (40%), Orthodox (2.2%)
Other faiths: Jews 3.2%, Muslim 1.1%, Hindu 0.2%, Buddhist 0.1%

The Episcopal Church, U.S.A.

Province 9, including Mexico and Central America, shown on separate map.

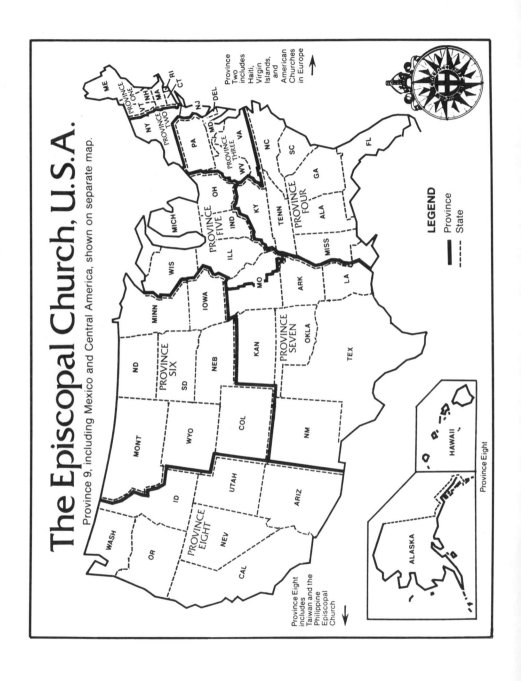

Province Two includes Haiti, Virgin Islands, and American Churches in Europe

Province Eight includes Taiwan and the Philippine Episcopal Church

LEGEND
— Province
---- State

Province Eight

USA, continued

Parishes: 7,409
Number of clergy: 14,111
Theological seminaries: 11 accredited Episcopal seminaries.

Brief history: The Church of England was brought to the New World by early explorers and colonists and during the 18th century was especially assisted by the SPCK and SPG. Anglicanism was the dominant church in the southern colonies such as Virginia (first celebration of the Holy Communion, Jamestown 1607) and strong in some parts of the north, but no resident bishop was provided for nearly 200 years and many of the clergy sided with the Crown during the American Revolution. After the Revolution, the church was slowly reorganized and rebuilt by state conventions (later dioceses), a series of national meetings and the securing of the Episcopate from England, thus forming the first Anglican Province independent from the Church of England. In 1784, Seabury of Connecticut, the first American bishop, was consecrated in Scotland. In 1785, the first General Convention was held, and in 1787 two more bishops were consecrated in England. In 1821, the Domestic and Foreign Missionary Society was organized. The Episcopal Church is governed by a triennial General Convention consisting of a House of Bishops, including all diocesan, suffragan, assistant and retired bishops and a House of (Clerical and Lay) Deputies elected by their dioceses. Between General Conventions, affairs are in the hands of an Executive Council, whose members are elected in part by the two Houses and in part by the regional provinces, and which meets several times a year.

Presiding Bishop: Edmond L. Browning
Provincial Office: 815 Second Ave., New York, NY, 10017
Provincial newspaper: *The Episcopalian*, monthly

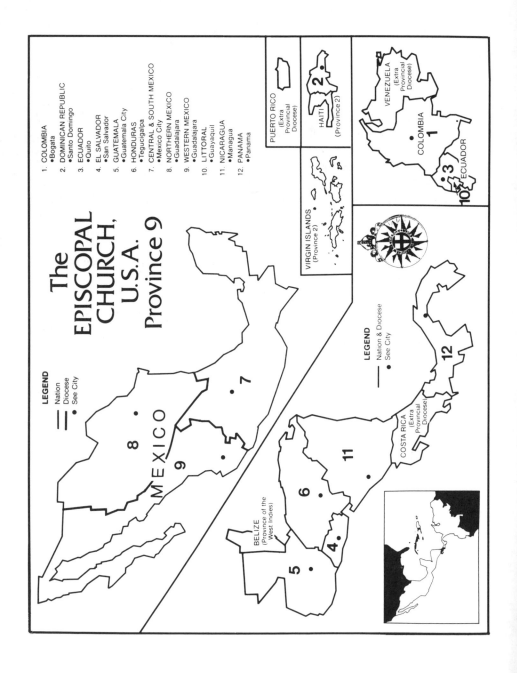

The
EPISCOPAL
CHURCH,
U.S.A.
Province 9

LEGEND
Nation
Diocese
● See City

1. COLOMBIA
   ● Bogata
2. DOMINICAN REPUBLIC
   ● Santo Domingo
3. ECUADOR
   ● Quito
4. EL SALVADOR
   ● San Salvador
5. GUATEMALA
   ● Guatemala City
6. HONDURAS
   ● Tegucigalpa
7. CENTRAL & SOUTH MEXICO
   ● Mexico City
8. NORTHERN MEXICO
   ● Guadalajara
9. WESTERN MEXICO
   ● Guadalajara
10. LITTORAL
    ● Guayaquil
11. NICARAGUA
    ● Managua
12. PANAMA
    ● Panama

PUERTO RICO
(Extra
Provincial
Diocese)

HAITI
(Province 2)

VENEZUELA
(Extra
Provincial
Diocese)

COLOMBIA
1

ECUADOR

3

10

VIRGIN ISLANDS
(Province 2)

LEGEND
Nation & Diocese
● See City

MEXICO

8

9

7

BELIZE
(Province of the
West Indies)

5

4

6

11

COSTA RICA
(Extra
Provincial
Diocese)

12

The Episcopal Church, Province 9
Central America and adjacent areas

Countries: Mexico, Guatemala, Honduras, El Salvador, Nicaragua, Panama,
The Dominican Republic, Colombia and Ecuador
Geographical area: 1,518,487 square miles
Population: est. 134,928,000
Number of Anglicans: 45,667 (1985)
Dioceses: 12 (Central and South Mexico, Colombia, Dominican Republic, Ecuador, El Salvador, Guatemala, Honduras, Littoral, Nicaragua, Northern Mexico, Panama, Western Mexico)
Number of Christians: est. 131,204,000
In the different countries, Roman Catholic membership varies from a low of 82% to a high of 98.3% of the population; Protestant figures vary from 0.1% to 5%.
Other faiths: In Panama there is a significant Muslim population (3.6%) and a growing Bahai movement.

Parishes: 259 (1985)
Number of clergy: 162 (1985)

Brief history: These former missionary districts of the Episcopal Church USA and parts of other Anglican missionary dioceses were formed into a regional province of ECUSA in 1964. Although the church in each country has its own history and distinctive features, they are all Spanish-speaking, most are of recent origin as separate dioceses, and most are built on the foundation of English speaking chaplaincies to expatriots or to immigrant workers from the West Indies and their descendants. The religious and cultural traditions of the region are overwhelmingly Roman Catholic, but Pentecostal and evangelical churches have grown rapidly in recent years. Mexico is an exception in that the Episcopal Church there has been indigenous from its beginnings as a nationalist secession from the Roman Catholic Church in 1857. The first Anglican bishop for Mexico was consecrated in 1879. Other dioceses with the dates of their founding are: Panama 1920, Dominican Republic 1940, Colombia 1964, Ecuador 1970, El Salvador 1968, Guatemala 1968, Honduras 1968, Nicaragua 1968. While they are now full members of the General Convention of the Episcopal Church USA, it is expected that dioceses from the region will soon form an autonomous Spanish speaking Province of the Anglican Communion.

The President of Province 9 is the Bishop of Panama, James Ottley, Box R, Balboa, Republic de Panama

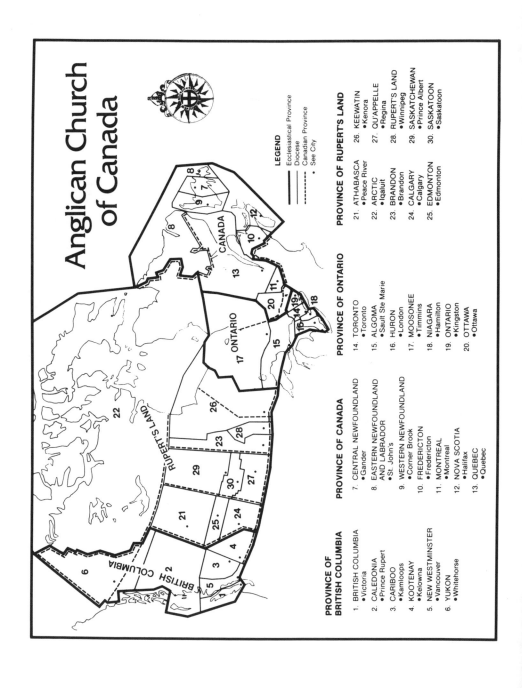

Anglican Church of Canada

LEGEND
― Ecclesiastical Province
― Diocese
- - - Canadian Province
• See City

PROVINCE OF BRITISH COLUMBIA
1. BRITISH COLUMBIA
   • Victoria
2. CALEDONIA
   • Prince Rupert
3. CARIBOO
   • Kamloops
4. KOOTENAY
   • Kelowna
5. NEW WESTMINSTER
   • Vancouver
6. YUKON
   • Whitehorse

PROVINCE OF CANADA
7. CENTRAL NEWFOUNDLAND
   • Gander
8. EASTERN NEWFOUNDLAND AND LABRADOR
   • St. John's
9. WESTERN NEWFOUNDLAND
   • Corner Brook
10. FREDERICTON
    • Fredericton
11. MONTREAL
    • Montreal
12. NOVA SCOTIA
    • Halifax
13. QUEBEC
    • Quebec

PROVINCE OF ONTARIO
14. TORONTO
    • Toronto
15. ALGOMA
    • Sault Ste Marie
16. HURON
    • London
17. MOOSONEE
    • Timmins
18. NIAGARA
    • Hamilton
19. ONTARIO
    • Kingston
20. OTTAWA
    • Ottawa

PROVINCE OF RUPERT'S LAND
21. ATHABASCA
    • Peace River
22. ARCTIC
    • Iqaluit
23. BRANDON
    • Brandon
24. CALGARY
    • Calgary
25. EDMONTON
    • Edmonton
26. KEEWATIN
    • Kenora
27. QU'APPELLE
    • Regina
28. RUPERT'S LAND
    • Winnipeg
29. SASKATCHEWAN
    • Prince Albert
30. SASKATOON
    • Saskatoon

The Anglican Church of Canada

Geographical area: 3,851,809 square miles
Population: 25,500,000
Number of Anglicans: 2,430,000 (census); 833,851 (parish rolls)
Dioceses: 30, grouped into four internal provinces
> *British Columbia:* British Columbia, Caledonia, Cariboo, Kootenay, New Westminster, Yukon. *Canada:* Central Newfoundland, Eastern Newfoundland and Labrador, Fredericton, Montreal, Nova Scotia, Quebec, Western Newfoundland. *Ontario:* Algoma, Huron, Moonsonee, Niagara, Ontario, Ottawa, Toronto. *Rupert's Land:* The Arctic, Athabasca, Brandon, Calgary, Edmonton, Keewatin, Qu'Appelle, Rupert's Land, Saskatchewan, Saskatoon

Number of Christians: 22,300,000
> Roman Catholic (46%), United Church (16.9%), Anglicans (10%)

Other faiths: Muslim (1.4%), Jews (0.6%), Baha'i (0.2%)

Parishes: 1,707
Number of clergy: 3,180
Theological colleges: 9

Brief history: The Anglican Church of Canada came into existence as the result of the work of British churches and missionary societies, particularly the USPG and CMS, which sent missionaries and teachers to the new land in the 18th and 19th centuries. First regular services began in 1710 at Port Royal; first church building, St. Paul's Halifax 1750; first bishop, Charles Inglis, Bishop of Nova Scotia 1787. Provincial Synod dates from the 1860s and General Synod from 1893. The Church includes in its membership large numbers of the original inhabitants of Canada—Indian, Eskimo and Metis—and has been a strong advocate of their rights.

Primate: Michael G. Peers
Provincial office: 600 Jarvis Street, Toronto, Ontario, Canada, M4Y 2J6
Provincial newspaper: *The Canadian Churchman*

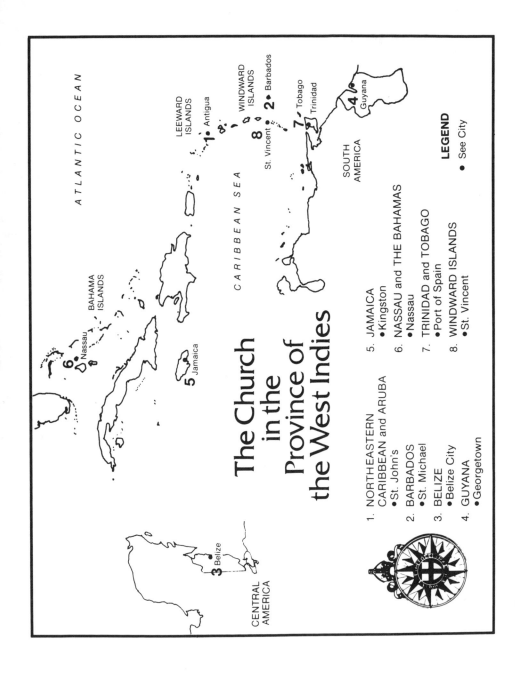

The Church in the Province of the West Indies

1. NORTHEASTERN CARIBBEAN and ARUBA
   • St. John's
2. BARBADOS
   • St. Michael
3. BELIZE
   • Belize City
4. GUYANA
   • Georgetown
5. JAMAICA
   • Kingston
6. NASSAU and THE BAHAMAS
   • Nassau
7. TRINIDAD and TOBAGO
   • Port of Spain
8. WINDWARD ISLANDS
   • St. Vincent

LEGEND
• See City

ATLANTIC OCEAN

CARIBBEAN SEA

CENTRAL AMERICA

SOUTH AMERICA

BAHAMA ISLANDS

LEEWARD ISLANDS

WINDWARD ISLANDS

Nassau
Jamaica
Belize
Antigua
St. Vincent
Barbados
Tobago
Trinidad
Guyana

The Church in the Province of the West Indies

Countries: Barbados, Belize, Guyana, Jamaica, Nassau and the Bahamas, Antigua, St. Lucia, St. Vincent, Grenada, Trinidad and Tobago, Dominica, St. Kitts, Nevis, Montserrat
Geographical area: 106,244 square miles
Population: 4,400,000
Number of Anglicans: 770,000
Dioceses: 8 (Barbados, Belize, Guyana, Jamaica, Nassau and the Bahamas, North Eastern Caribbean and Aruba, Trinidad and Tobago, Windward Islands)
Number of Christians: 4,100,000
    Protestant (32%), Roman Catholic (26%)
Other faiths: Hindu (3%)

Parishes: 892
Number of clergy: 368

Brief history: The Church of England established mission stations in various West Indies territories that became British colonies. In 1883 the Church in the Province of the West Indies was formally established, including a Provincial Synod. In 1897 the Most Rev. Enos Nuttall became the first Archbishop of the West Indies. In 1976 Trinidad hosted the third meeting of the Anglican Consultative Council.

Archbishop: Orland U. Lindsay
Provincial Secretary: The Rt. Rev. K. A. McMillan, The Bishop of Belize, Bishopsthorpe, Southern Foreshore, P.O. Box 535, Belize City, Belize, West Indies
Provincial newspaper: *CARIBBEAN CONTACT,* P.O. Box 616, Bridgetown, Barbados, West Indies

Dioceses in Central America and the Caribbean

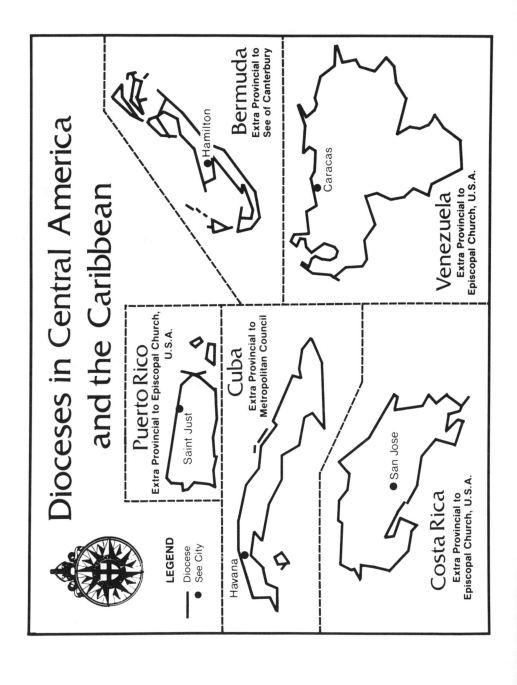

LEGEND
— Diocese
• See City

Bermuda
Extra Provincial to
See of Canterbury

• Hamilton

Venezuela
Extra Provincial to
Episcopal Church, U.S.A.

• Caracas

Puerto Rico
Extra Provincial to Episcopal Church,
U.S.A.

• Saint Just

Cuba
Extra Provincial to
Metropolitan Council

• Havana

Costa Rica
Extra Provincial to
Episcopal Church, U.S.A.

• San Jose

44

Extra-Provincial Dioceses

Bermuda: Extra-provincial to Canterbury. Bermuda was first colonized by Anglicans from Great Britain in 1609 and within a few years 9 parishes were established, each with its own church. Until 1813 the church was under the Bishop of London, then, until 1917, under the Bishop of Newfoundland. Since 1925 it has been under the direct jurisdiction of the Archbishop of Canterbury. There are today 25,000 members (42% of the population) in 17 congregations. Two thirds of the population are Black, 98% are Christian. After the Anglican Church, the major churches are Protestant (26%) and Roman Catholic (18%).

Cuba: Under the Spanish Empire, Cuba became Roman Catholic. The Spanish-American War of 1898 opened the country to the work of other churches. It became a missionary district of the Episcopal Church USA in 1901. Cuba received its first missionary bishop in 1904, its first Cuban bishop in 1961. Since 1966 Cuba has been an autonomous diocese under a metropolitan council made up of the primates of the West Indies and Canada and the president of Province 9, USA. An estimated 3,000 active members (many having emigrated to the USA) in 42 parishes served by 13 clergy, make up 0.1% of the population.

Costa Rica: Extra-provincial diocese, related to Province 9, USA, 5,000 members, 14 clergy in a predominantly Roman Catholic population estimated at 2,286,000. Anglican contacts and occasional services from 1837. Under Bishop of Belize (British Honduras) from 1896. Under Episcopal Church USA since 1947. J. A. Ramos of Cuba elected first hispanic bishop of Costa Rica in 1968; the diocese became independent soon after.

Puerto Rico. Extra-provincial diocese related to Province 9, USA. First missions established among West Indian migrant workers by the Bishop of Antigua in the 1860s. Following the Spanish-American War the island became an American dependency, and in 1901, a domestic missionary district of the Episcopal Church. Election of first Puerto Rican bishop in 1964. Partly as a result of local agitation for either statehood or independence, the diocese sought and obtained autonomy from the American church, but continues to work as closely as possible with that church and with Spanish speaking Anglican neighbors. The island is 92% Roman Catholic. 15,000 Anglicans in 40 parishes served by 49 clergy, make up 0.4% of the population.

Venezuela. Extra-provincial diocese of Province 9, USA. Chaplaincies for English speaking residents since 1830s. In the 1960s Canadian Anglicans started missionary work and Venezuela in 1976 became a diocese in the Province of the West Indies. Spanish speaking congregations were begun and in 1981 the first Venezuelan priest was ordained. In 1982 the diocese was transferred to the 9th province of the Episcopal Church with extra-provincial status. There are approximately 1,000 Anglicans in 8 parishes served by 11 clergy.

The (Anglican) Council of
Churches of East Asia

Pending the establishment of new Provinces, the Council serves as a link between the churches and dioceses in Burma (5 dioceses), the Philippines (4 dioceses), Korea (3 dioceses), Hong Kong and Macao, Kuching (Borneo), Sabah, Singapore, Taiwan and West Malaysia.

Burma is an independent Province, Taiwan and the Philippine Episcopal Church are part of Province 8, USA, and the rest are extra-provincial dioceses under the Archbishop of Canterbury. The Philippine Independent Church and the Anglican Church of Australia are also members of the Council.

The Episcopal Church in Korea. Founded by USPG missionaries within the last century, the church now includes an estimated 53,000 members in 3 dioceses and more than 70 congregations, all presently in South Korea. It is a minority church in a traditionally Buddhist country with a rapidly growing Christian population of many denominations, mainly Presbyterian and Methodist. Roman Catholics also claim 1,400,000 members or about 4% of the population.

Hong Kong and Macao, established in 1843, once included most of South China, within the Anglican Church in China (Chung Hua Sheng Kung Hui). The diocese was subdivided during and after World War II. More than 50 clergy minister to 29,000 members. The diocese has maintained a large system of schools and social service centers and has supplied many leaders to Chinese communities in other countries.

Taiwan. Before World War II there were congregations of Japanese Anglicans on the island. Work was begun again in 1949 under the Bishop of Hawaii in response to the need for pastoral care of Chinese Anglicans who had left the mainland. It became an independent diocese in 1965 and now has 23 clergy and more than 1,000 members.

Singapore. Anglican chaplaincy from 1826. SPG missionaries from 1856. Diocese was founded in 1909. It has served as a center for theological training and for evangelism among Malaysian and other peoples of the region.

West Malaysia (1970) and **Kuching** and **Sabah** (1962) in North Borneo, were established to strengthen the work of evangelism in predominantly Muslim areas and among adherents of indigenous religions. Sabah, for example, now includes 15,000 Anglicans in 19 parishes with 21 clergy.

Church of the Province of Burma
Myanmanainggan Karityan Athindaw

Geographical area: 261,789 square miles
Population: 29,000,000
Number of Anglicans: 42,000
Dioceses: 5 (Mandalay, Myitkyina, Pa'an, Rangoon, Sittwe)
Number of Christians: 1,900,000
        Roman Catholic (3%), Protestants, mainly Baptist, (4%)
Other faiths: Buddhist (87%), Muslim (4%), Traditional (2%)

Parishes: 150
Number of clergy:

Brief history: Anglican chaplains from 1825, USPG missionaries 1859-1966. First diocese, Rangoon, established 1877; it continued as part of the Church of India, Pakistan, Burma and Ceylon until the India and Pakistan dioceses were incorporated in united churches. The Church of the Province of Burma was inaugurated in 1970. In 1961 Buddhism was declared the State religion. In 1966 all foreign missionaries were forced to leave. On its own resources and under many difficulties the Church has continued steady growth.

Archbishop:
Provincial office: Bishopscourt, 140 Pyidaungsu-Yeiktha Road. Dagon P.O. (11191),
        Rangoon, Burma
Provincial magazine: *The Newsletter*

Philippine Episcopal Church

1. CENTRAL PHILIPPINES
   • Quezon City
2. NORTHERN LUZON
   • Bulanao
3. NORTHERN PHILIPPINES
   • Boutoc
4. SOUTHERN PHILIPPINES
   • Cotabato City

The Council of Churches in East Asia

Extra Provincial to See of Canterbury

1. HONG KONG and MACAO
   • Hong Kong
2. KUCHING (BORNEO)
   • Kuching, Sarawak
3. PUSAN
   • Pusan
4. SABAH
   • Sabah
5. SEOUL
   • Seoul
6. SINGAPORE
   • Singapore
7. TAEJON
   • Taejon
8. WEST MALAYSIA
   • Kuala Lumpur

LEGEND

Nation
Diocese
• See City

Province of Burma

1. AKYAB
   • Akyab
2. MANDALAY
   • Mandalay
3. MYITKYINA
   • Myitkyina
4. PAAN
   • Toungoo
5. RANGOON
   • Rangoon

Church in Sri Lanka

1. COLOMBO
   • Colombo
2. KURUNAGALA
   • Kurunagala

48

The Church in Sri Lanka

Geographical area: 25,332 square miles
Population: 16,500,000
Number of Anglicans: 55,000
Dioceses: 2 (Colombo, Kurunagala)
Number of Christians: 1,200,000
      Roman Catholic: 7% of the population and 88% of all Christians
Other faiths: Buddhist (67%), Hindu (16%), Muslim (7%)

Parishes: 130
Number of clergy: 110

Brief history: Until 1970 part of the Church of India, Pakistan, Burma and Ceylon. First Anglican services in 1796. CMS missionaries from 1818. The two dioceses have planned to become part of a united Church of Lanka, a plan frustrated thus far by legal problems and civil strife. They continue as extra-provincial dioceses under the Archbishop of Canterbury.

Provincial office: 368/1 Bauddlaloka Mawatha, Colombo 7, Sri Lanka

The Philippine Episcopal Church

Geographical area: 115,830 square miles
Population: 52,200,000
Number of Anglicans: 86,100
Dioceses: 4 (Central, Northern, Southern Philippines, Northern Luzon,
Number of Christians: 49,200,000
          Roman Catholic (89%), Protestant (3%)
Other faiths: Muslim (4.3%), traditional (0.7%)

Parishes: 125
Number of clergy: 140
Theological college: St. Andrew's Theological Seminary, Manila

Brief history: As a Spanish colony since the 16th century, the Philippines became predominantly Roman Catholic. When the islands became an American colony in 1898, Bishop Charles Henry Brent of the USA established missionary work among the largely unevangelized tribespeople of Northern Luzon and among Muslim populations in the South. The missionary diocese of the Philippines was established in 1901. In 1971 and later the area was subdivided into four dioceses. The first Philippine bishop, E. G. Longid, was consecrated in 1963 and the church hopes to become an independent Province in 1989. Meanwhile it enjoys close working relationships with the Philippine Independent Church. All four dioceses are members of the General Convention of the Episcopal Church USA and part of Province 8 of that church.

Presiding Bishop: Manuel C. Lumpias, Bishop of Central Philippines, P.O. Box
      655, Manila, Philippines
Provincial office: c/o The Episcopal Church Center, 815 Second Avenue, New
      York, New York 10017

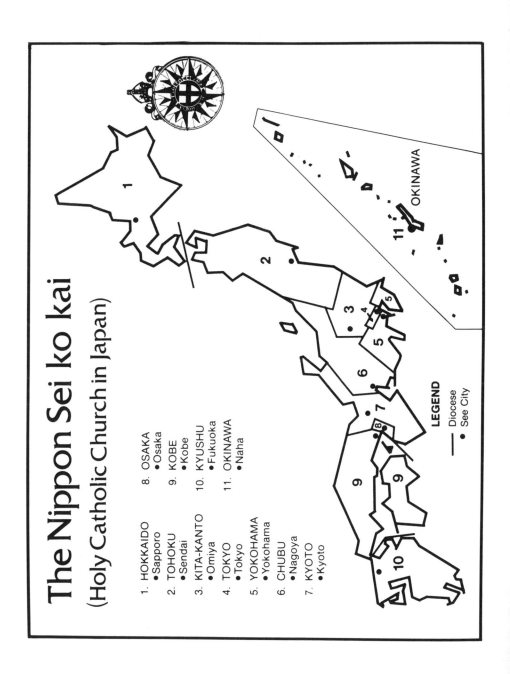

The Nippon Sei ko kai
(Holy Catholic Church in Japan)

1. HOKKAIDO
   • Sapporo
2. TOHOKU
   • Sendai
3. KITA-KANTO
   • Omiya
4. TOKYO
   • Tokyo
5. YOKOHAMA
   • Yokohama
6. CHUBU
   • Nagoya
7. KYOTO
   • Kyoto

8. OSAKA
   • Osaka
9. KOBE
   • Kobe
10. KYUSHU
    • Fukuoka
11. OKINAWA
    • Naha

LEGEND
— Diocese
• See City

The Holy Catholic Church in Japan
Nippon Sei Ko Kai (N.S.K.K.)

Geographical area: 126,000 square miles
Population: 120,000,000
Number of Anglicans: 60,000
Dioceses: 11 (Chubu, Hokkaido, Kita-Kanto, Kobe, Kyoto, Kyushu, Okinawa,
    Osaka, Tohoku, Tokyo, Yokohama)
Number of Christians: 1,111,000 (0.8%)
Other faiths: Buddhist (73%), Shinto (12.5%), Other (13.3%)

Congregations: 316
Number of clergy: 350
Theological colleges: Central Theological College in Tokyo; Bishop William's
    Memorial Seminary, Kyoto

Brief history: In 1859, the American Episcopal Church sent two missionaries from China to open new work in Japan. They were later joined by missionaries from England and Canada. A general Anglican Synod took place in 1887, adopted the constitution, canons and Prayer Book for the Province and unified the work of the various Anglican missionary societies. Its first Japanese bishops were consecrated in 1923. During World War II the church remained underground rather than comply with government decrees. After the war all responsibility for the life of the church and its many educational and medical institutions was assumed by Japanese leadership and increasing assistance has been given from Japan to other parts of the Anglican Communion. The Province is governed by a triennial General Synod including a House of Bishops and a House of Clergy and Lay deputies. The Primate is elected from among the active bishops for a three year term.

Primate: Christopher Kikawada
Provincial office: 4-21 Higashi 1-chome, Shibuya-ku, Tokyo, 150, Japan
Provincial newspaper: *Sei Ko Kai Shimbun*, monthly

The Church of England

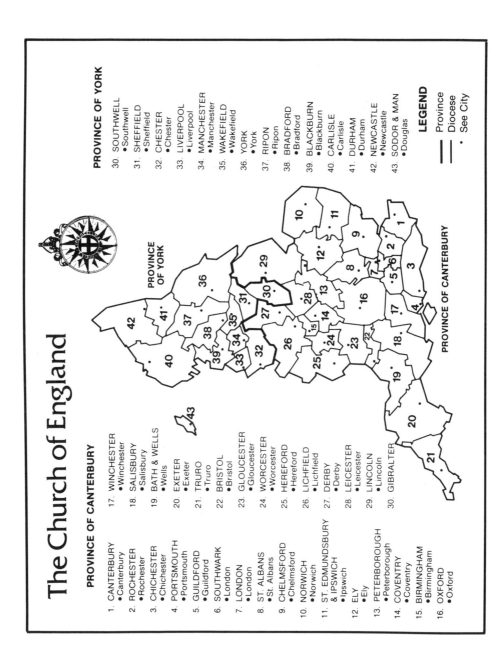

PROVINCE OF CANTERBURY

1. CANTERBURY
   • Canterbury
2. ROCHESTER
   • Rochester
3. CHICHESTER
   • Chichester
4. PORTSMOUTH
   • Portsmouth
5. GUILDFORD
   • Guildford
6. SOUTHWARK
   • London
7. LONDON
   • London
8. ST. ALBANS
   • St. Albans
9. CHELMSFORD
   • Chelmsford
10. NORWICH
    • Norwich
11. ST. EDMUNDSBURY
    & IPSWICH
    • Ipswich
12. ELY
    • Ely
13. PETERBOROUGH
    • Peterborough
14. COVENTRY
    • Coventry
15. BIRMINGHAM
    • Birmingham
16. OXFORD
    • Oxford
17. WINCHESTER
    • Winchester
18. SALISBURY
    • Salisbury
19. BATH & WELLS
    • Wells
20. EXETER
    • Exeter
21. TRURO
    • Truro
22. BRISTOL
    • Bristol
23. GLOUCESTER
    • Gloucester
24. WORCESTER
    • Worcester
25. HEREFORD
    • Hereford
26. LICHFIELD
    • Lichfield
27. DERBY
    • Derby
28. LEICESTER
    • Leicester
29. LINCOLN
    • Lincoln
30. GIBRALTAR

PROVINCE OF YORK

30. SOUTHWELL
    • Southwell
31. SHEFFIELD
    • Sheffield
32. CHESTER
    • Chester
33. LIVERPOOL
    • Liverpool
34. MANCHESTER
    • Manchester
35. WAKEFIELD
    • Wakefield
36. YORK
    • York
37. RIPON
    • Ripon
38. BRADFORD
    • Bradford
39. BLACKBURN
    • Blackburn
40. CARLISLE
    • Carlisle
41. DURHAM
    • Durham
42. NEWCASTLE
    • Newcastle
43. SODOR & MAN
    • Douglas

LEGEND

—— Province
- - - Diocese
• See City

The Church of England

Countries: England, very small part of Wales
Geographical area: 50,705 square miles
Population: 47,318,000
Number of Anglicans: 1,559,300 (1985 Electoral roll). Approximately 25,000,000
    baptized members
Dioceses: 44, in two provinces, Canterbury and York.
    Canterbury: Bath and Wells, Birmingham, Bristol, Canterbury, Chelms-
    ford, Chichester, Coventry, Derby, Ely, Europe, Exeter, Gloucester,
    Guildford, Hereford, Leicester, Lichfield, Lincoln, London, Norwich,
    Oxford, Peterborough, Portsmouth, Rochester, St. Albans, St. Ed-
    mundsbury & Ipswich, Salisbury, Southwark, Truro, Winchester,
    Worcester. *York:* Blackburn, Bradford, Carlisle, Chester, Durham,
    Liverpool, Manchester, Newcastle, Ripon, Sheffield, Sodor and Man,
    Southwell, Wakefield, York
Number of Christians: 87% of population
    Roman Catholic (15%), Protestant (13%)
Other faiths: Muslim (1.4%), Jews (0.8%), Hindu (0.7%)

Parishes: 13,287
Number of clergy: 10,624 (full-time stipendiary)
Theological colleges: 14—Queens, Trinity, Ridley Hall, Westcott House,
    Chichester, Ripon, Lincoln, Oak Hill, St. Stephen's House, Wycliffe
    Hall, Salisbury and Wells, Cranmer Hall, Mirfield, St. John's and 15
    part-time courses.

Brief history: See pages 3, 4. The Church of England is governed by a General
Synod consisting of the Convocations of Canterbury and York joined together
in a House of Bishops and a House of Clergy and having added to them a House
of Laity (elected from the Deanery Synods). The 574 members of General Synod meet at least twice a year and the Archbishops of Canterbury and York serve
as joint Presidents.

Archbishop of Canterbury: Robert A. K. Runcie
Archbishop of York: John S. Habgood
Provincial Office: Church House, Dean's Yard, London SW1P 3NZ, England
Provincial newspapers: *Church Times, Church of England Newspaper,* and others.

Church
of
Ireland

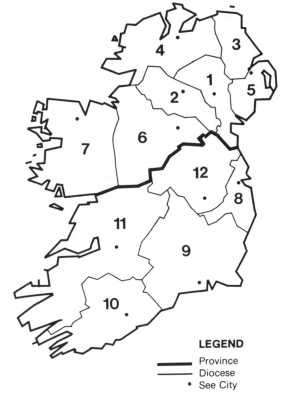

LEGEND

▬▬▬ Province
─── Diocese
• See City

PROVINCE OF ARMAGH

1. ARMAGH
   • Armagh
2. CLOGHER
   • Fivemiletown
3. CONNOR
   • Belfast
4. DERRY AND RAPHOE
   • Londonderry
5. DOWN AND DROMORE
   • South Belfast
6. KILMORE, ELPHIN AND ARDAGH
   • Cavan
7. TUAM KILLALA AND ACHONRY
   • Crossmolina

PROVINCE OF DUBLIN

8. DUBLIN AND GLENDALOUGH
   • Dublin
9. CASHEL AND OSSORY
   • Waterford
10. CORK CLOYNE AND ROSS
    • Cork
11. LIMERICK AND KILLALOE
    • Limerick
12. MEATH AND KILDARE
    • Kildare

The Church of Ireland
Eaglais na hEireann

Countries: The Republic of Ireland and Northern Ireland
Geographical area: 32,597 square miles
Population: 4,925,000
Number of Anglicans: 410,000
Dioceses: 12, grouped in provinces of Armagh and Dublin *Armagh:* Armagh;
    Clogher; Connor; Derry and Raphoe; Down and Dromore; Kilmore,
    Elphin and Ardagh; Tuam, Killala and Achonry. *Dublin:* Cashel and
    Ossory; Cork, Cloyne and Ross; Dublin and Glendalough; Limerick
    and Killaloe; Meath and Kildare
Number of Christians: 4,800,000
    Roman Catholic (70%), Protestant (20%)
Other faiths: .005%

Parishes: about 1,150
Number of clergy: 650
Theological college: The Church of Ireland Theological College, Dublin

Brief history: Christianity in Ireland traces it origin to St. Patrick and his companions in the 5th century and from the beginning until now, Irish churches have been marked by strong missionary zeal. In 1537 the English king was declared head of the Church of Ireland and submission to Roman authority was forbidden. While Anglicanism thus received state support, most Irish Christians identified patriotism with continued loyalty to Rome. In 1867 the Anglican Church in Ireland was dis-established and continued as an independent Province, centered mainly in the north. It is governed by a General Synod with a House of Bishops and a House of Representatives (clergy and laity). The Primate, the Archbishop of Armagh, is elected by the House of Bishops from their own number.

Primate: The Archbishop of Armagh, Robert H. A. Eames
Provincial office: Church of Ireland House, Church Avenue, Rathmines,
    Dublin, 6, Ireland
Provincial newspaper: *Church of Ireland Gazette*, weekly

The Scottish Episcopal Church

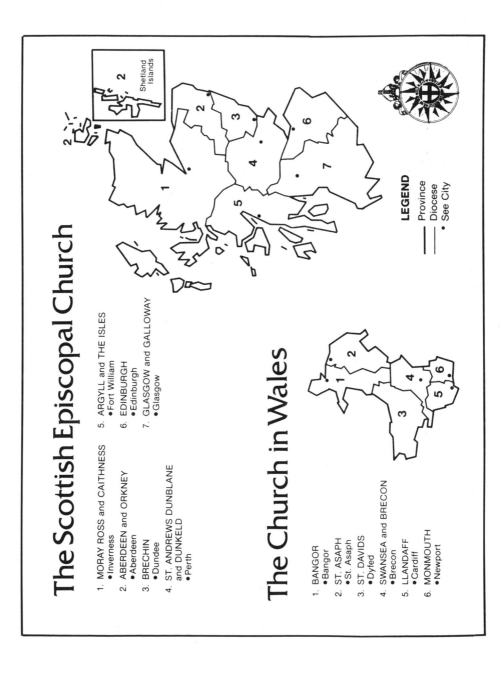

1. MORAY ROSS and CAITHNESS
   ● Inverness

2. ABERDEEN and ORKNEY
   ● Aberdeen

3. BRECHIN
   ● Dundee

4. ST. ANDREWS DUNBLANE
   and DUNKELD
   ● Perth

5. ARGYLL and THE ISLES
   ● Fort William

6. EDINBURGH
   ● Edinburgh

7. GLASGOW and GALLOWAY
   ● Glasgow

LEGEND
—— Province
—— Diocese
● See City

The Church in Wales

1. BANGOR
   ● Bangor

2. ST. ASAPH
   ● St. Asaph

3. ST. DAVIDS
   ● Dyfed

4. SWANSEA and BRECON
   ● Brecon

5. LLANDAFF
   ● Cardiff

6. MONMOUTH
   ● Newport

Scottish Episcopal Church

Geographical area: 30,414 square miles
Population: 5,000,000
Number of Anglicans: 60,000
Dioceses: 7 (Aberdeen and Orkney; Argyll and the Isles; Brechin; Edinburgh; Glasgow and Galloway; Moray, Ross and Caithness; St. Andrews, Dunkeld and Dunblane)
Number of Christians: 2,000,000
Presbyterian (50%), Roman Catholic (40%)

Parishes: 280
Number of clergy: 200 stipendiary, 100 non-stipendiary
Theological colleges: Edinburgh

Brief History: The roots of Christianity in Scotland go back to Ninian in the fourth century and Columba in the sixth century. After the Reformation, between 1560 and 1689, sometimes the Episcopal Church, sometimes the Presbyterian Church was "Established." Following 1689 until the early nineteenth century, the Episcopal Church was weakened by Penal Statutes and disestablishment. It grew rapidly in the nineteenth century, influenced by the Tractarian Movement. There has been a slow decline of numbers in the twentieth century. The Church is numerically stronger in the East than in the West. In 1982 the Church adopted a system of government by General Synod which meets annually. The seven bishops elect one of their number as Primus, who is recognized as spokesman for the Church.

Primus: Edward Luscombe
Provincial office: 21 Grosvenor Crescent, Edinburgh EH12 5EE, Scotland
Provincial newspaper: *NEWSCAN*

The Church in Wales
Eglwys yng Nghymru

Geographical area: 8,006 square miles
Population: 2,807,800
Number of Anglicans: 115,947 (Easter Communicants in 1987)
Dioceses: 6 (Bangor, Llandaff, Monmouth, St. Asaph, St. David's, Swansea and
        Brecon)
Number of Christians: 500,875 (1985), predominantly Roman Catholic, Anglican
        and Presbyterian

Parishes: 1,122
Number of clergy: 760
Theological college: St. Michael's College, Llandaff, Cardiff

Brief history: The Church in Wales was disestablished, i.e. became a separate
province on April 1, 1920. The first Archbishop was enthroned on June 1 of
that year. The Church is governed by its Governing Body, a synod of bishops,
clergy and laity which meets twice a year. Property is held and finances administered by the Representative Body.

Archbishop: George Noakes
Provincial office: 39 Cathedral Road, Cardiff, CF1 9XF, Wales
Provincial newspaper: *Y Llan, Welsh Churchman*

Portugal and Spain

SPAIN

• Madrid

PORTUGAL

SPANISH REFORMED EPISCOPAL CHURCH

(Extra–provincial to Canterbury)

Lisbon •

LUSITANIAN CHURCH
(Extra–provincial to Canterbury)

• Gibraltar in Europe
(Province of Canterbury)

The Diocese in Europe (Gibraltar); Province of Canterbury. The diocese is responsible for the Church of England chaplaincies and organized congregations throughout the whole of continental Europe, from Norway to Russia, Greece to the Azores and including Turkey and Morocco. The Cathedral is in Gibraltar, with Pro-Cathedrals also in Malta and Brussels. The diocese was organized in its present form in 1980. From 1841 the Bishop of Gibraltar had been in charge of the same territory under the Bishop of London.

The Convocation of American Churches in Europe consists of six congregations in Western Europe, including a Pro-Cathedral in Paris, under the jurisdiction of the Presiding Bishop of the Episcopal Church USA and administered by a bishop appointed by him. The American bishop cooperates closely with the Bishop of Gibraltar in Europe and with the American Suffragan for the Armed Forces.

Lusitanian Church (The Portuguese Episcopal Church) since 1980 an extra-provincial diocese under the Archbishop of Canterbury. This small church was first organized in 1880 by a group of dissident Roman Catholic priests and laymen, with the help of the Episcopal Bishop of Mexico and with the intention of becoming part of the Anglican Communion. Subsequently, episcopal supervision, confirmations and ordinations were provided by a Council of Bishops from the Church of Ireland. The first Portuguese bishop was consecrated in 1958. In the 1960s full communion was established with the Episcopal Church USA, Ireland, England and other Anglican Provinces. In 1980, the diocese became a full member of the Anglican Communion. There are an estimated 850 members in 12 congregations, served by 2 bishops and 10 other clergy.

The Spanish Reformed Episcopal Church, since 1980 an extra-provincial diocese under the Archbishop of Canterbury, has had a history similar to that of the Lusitanian Church, with its beginnings among former Roman Catholics in the 19th century and a long period of informal relations with certain bishops of the Church of Ireland. After its organization as a diocese and the consecration of its first bishop, the church entered into full communion in 1963 and into full membership in 1980 with the Anglican Communion. It has an estimated 1,200 members in 15 congregations served by 14 clergy. It sponsors, with other Evangelical bodies, a seminary in Madrid and has growing cooperation with the English speaking Anglican community in Spain of nearly 12,000 members, attached to the Dioese of Gibralter in Europe.

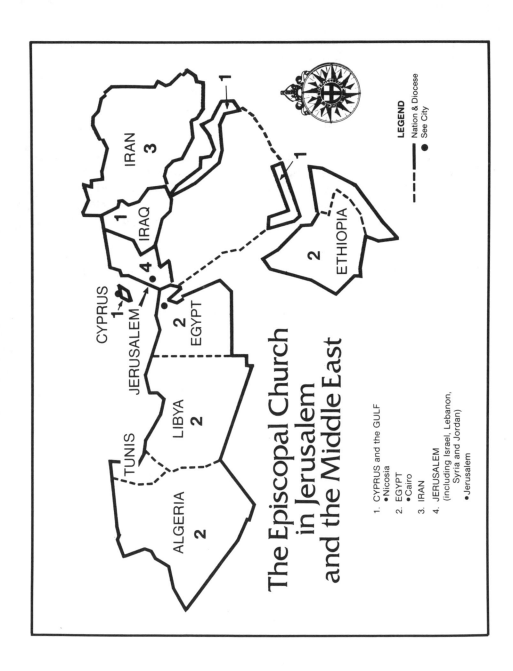

The Episcopal Church
in Jerusalem
and the Middle East

1. CYPRUS and the GULF
   ● Nicosia
2. EGYPT
   ● Cairo
3. IRAN
4. JERUSALEM
   (including Israel, Lebanon,
   Syria and Jordan)
   ● Jerusalem

LEGEND
——— Nation & Diocese
● See City

The Episcopal Church in Jerusalem and the Middle East

Countries: Israel, Jordan, Lebanon, Syria, Iran, Egypt, Libya, Tunisia, Algeria, Ethiopia, the Horn of Africa and Cyprus
Geographical area: 3,207,000 square miles
Population: 152,000,000 estimate
Number of Anglicans: 30,000
Dioceses: 4 (Cyprus and the Gulf, Egypt, Iran, Jerusalem)
Number of Christians: 28,803,500, predominantly Orthodox and Oriental Churches
Other faiths: Muslim, the overwhelming majority in the region as a whole, with local exceptions such as Cyprus, Israel and Lebanon

Congregations: 55 estimate
Number of clergy: 77 (29 indigenous, 12 expatriate, 36 expatriate chaplains)

Brief history: The Jerusalem Bishopric was founded in 1841 and became an Archbishopric in 1957. Its primary mission was to form links of friendship with the ancient churches of the area and to provide chaplaincy service to expatriate communities. There was also a slow but steady growth of missionary work among Palestinian Christians and various non-Christian populations, supported by CMS and other missionary societies. The Province was founded in 1976, as part of a general reorganization of Anglican work into four dioceses, linked together for mutual support and to further the indigenization of the church. It is governed by a Central Synod, under a President Bishop who is elected for a five year term. President Bishop: Samir Kafity, Bishop in Jerusalem, St. George's Close, P.O. Box 1248, Jerusalem, Israel

Anglican Church of Australia

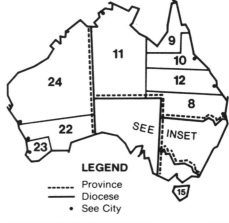

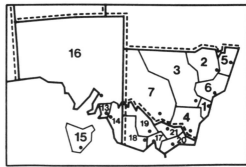

PROVINCE OF NEW SOUTH WALES

1. SYDNEY
   • Sidney
2. ARMIDALE
   • Armidale
3. BATHURST
   • Bathurst
4. CANBERRA & GOULBURN
   • Canberra
5. GRAFTON
   • Grafton
6. NEWCASTLE
   • Newcastle
7. RIVERINA
   • Narrandera

PROVINCE OF QUEENSLAND

8. BRISBANE
   • Bribane
9. CARPENTARIA
   • Thursday Island
10. N. QUEENSLAND
    • Townsville
11. NORTHERN TERRITORY
    • Darwin
12. ROCKHAMPTON
    • Rockhampton

LEGEND

- - - - - Province
———— Diocese
• See City

PROVINCE OF SOUTH AUSTRALIA

13. ADELAIDE
    • Adelaide
14. THE MURRAY
    • Murray Bridge
15. TASMANIA
    • Hobart
16. WILLOCHRA
    • Gladstone

PROVINCE OF VICTORIA

17. MELBOURNE
    • Melbourne
18. BALLARAT
    • Ballarat
19. BENDIGO
    • Bendigo
20. GIPPSLAND
    • Sale
21. WANGARATTA
    • Wangaratta

PROVINCE OF WESTERN AUSTRALIA

22. PERTH
    • Perth
23. BUNBURY
    • Bunbury
24. NORTHWEST AUSTRALIA
    • Geraldton

The Church of England in Australia

Geographical area: 2,967,000 square miles
Population: 15,602,156
Number of Anglicans: 3,723,419
Dioceses: 24, grouped into 5 internal provinces
> *Province of New South Wales:* Armidale, Bathurst, Canberra and Goulburn, Grafton, Newcastle, Riverina, Sydney. *Province of Queensland:* Brisbane, Carpentaria, North Queensland, Northern Territory, Rockhampton. *Province of South Australia:* Adelaide, The Murray, Willochra. *Province of Victoria:* Ballarat, Bendigo, Gippsland, Melbourne, Wangaratta. *Province of Western Australia:* Bunbury, North West Australia, Perth; *Extra-Provincial:* Tasmania

Number of Christians: 11,381,908
> Roman Catholics (26.1%), Uniting Church of Australia, (7.6%), Presbyterian (3.6%), Orthodox (2.7%), Baptist (1.3%), Lutheran (1.3%), Other (6.0%)

Other faiths: Atheists and non-religious (15%), Jews (0.5%), Muslim (0.7%)

Congregations: 1,400
Number of clergy: 2,400
Theological colleges: 10

Brief history: Anglicanism came to Australia with the "First Fleet" of convicts and their guards in 1788 and it grew with the establishment of other settlements as a colonial extension of the Church of England, although with growing autonomy, until 1962 when it became an independent Anglican Province. In 1824 the whole continent was an archdeaconry of the Bishop of Calcutta. In 1836, Broughton was consecrated the first Bishop of Australia. The subsequent development of new dioceses led to the first General Synod in 1872. The 20th century has been marked by continued growth of membership until recently, by the development of missionary work among aborigines and in adjacent Pacific islands and elsewhere; by the consolidation of regional provinces and the adoption of an Australian Prayer Book in 1978.

Archbishop and Primate: John Grindrod
Provincial office: P.O. Box Q190, Queen Victoria P.O., Sydney 2000, NSW, Australia
Provincial newspaper: *Church Scene,* independent weekly

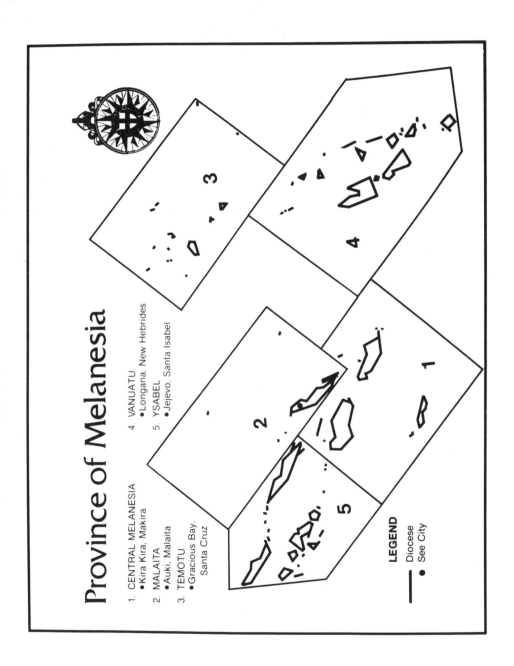

Province of Melanesia

1. CENTRAL MELANESIA
   • Kira Kira, Makira

2. MALAITA
   • Auki, Malaita

3. TEMOTU
   • Gracious Bay,
     Santa Cruz

4. VANUATU
   • Longana, New Hebrides

5. YSABEL
   • Jejevo, Santa Isabel

LEGEND
— Diocese
• See City

Church of the Province of Melanesia

Countries: Solomon Islands, Vanuatu, New Caledonia
Geographical area: 16,683 square miles
Population: 443,000
Number of Anglicans: 88,000
Dioceses: 5 (Central Melanesia, Malaita, Temotu, Vanuatu, Ysabel)
Number of Christians: 275,000
        Roman Catholics (14%), Protestants (30%), Melanesian indigenous
        (4%)
Other faiths: traditional (4%)

Parishes: (Districts) 95 estimated
Number of clergy: 185 estimated
Theological college: Bishop Patteson Theological Centre

Brief history: The Anglican presence in Melanesia dates from 1849 when George Selwyn, first bishop of New Zealand, toured the islands and brought back some young Melanesians to his school in Auckland. John Patteson became the first bishop of Melanesia in 1861 and was murdered ten years later, probably as a result of blackbirding activities. The first Mission in Melanesia Headquarters was on Norfolk Island. Permanent stations were set up in Melanesia in the 1880s. The Melanesian Brotherhood was founded in 1925. The autonomous Province was founded in 1975.

Archbishop: Amos S. Waiaru
Provincial office: P.O. Box 19, Honiaru, Solomon Islands.
Provincial newspaper/magazine: *Church of Melanesia*

Province of New Zealand

1. AUCKLAND
   - Torbey
2. CHRISTCHURCH
   - Christchurch
3. DUNEDIN
   - Dunedin
4. BISHOPRIC OF AOTEAROA
   - Rotorua
5. NELSON
   - Nelson
6. POLYNESIA
   - Suva, Fiji Islands
7. WAIAPU
   - Napier, Hawkes Bay
8. WAIKATO
   - Hamilton
9. WELLINGTON
   - Wellington

SAMOA

TONGA

FIJI ISLANDS

LEGEND
— Diocese
• See City

The Church of the Province of New Zealand

Countries: New Zealand, Fiji, Tonga, Western Samoa, Cook Islands
Geographical area: 103,747 square miles
Population: 3,200,000
Number of Anglicans: 200,000
Dioceses: 9 (Auckland, Christchurch, Dunedin, Nelson, Polynesia, To Pi-
hopatanga O Aotearoa, Waiapu, Waikato, Wellington)
Number of Christians: 600,000
Presbyterian (18%), Roman Catholic (16%)
Other faiths: 2%

Parishes: 360
Number of clergy: 800
Theological colleges: St. John's College, Selwyn College

Brief history: Began with a CMS mission to the Maori people in early 19th century. Settler church began alongside the Maori church in 1852. Governed by
General Synod—of three orders— meeting every two years. Current thrust: mission and evangelism as expressed by equal partnership and bi-cultural development, stemming from terms of Treaty of Waitangi at the founding of the nation.

Archbishop: Brian Davis
Provincial office: P.O. Box 2148, Rotorua, New Zealand

Province of Papua New Guinea

1. AIPO RONGO
   • Madang
2. DOGURA
   • Dogura Alotua
3. NEW GUINEA ISLANDS
   • Rabaul
4. POPONDOTA
   • Popondetta
5. PORT MORESBY
   • Port Moresby

LEGEND
— Diocese
• See City

The Anglican Church of Papua New Guinea

Countries: Papua New Guinea (19 states)
Geographical area: 178,703 square miles
Population: 3,397,000 (1986)
Number of Anglicans: 183,440
Dioceses: 5 (Aipo Rongo, Dogura, New Guinea Islands, Port Moresby, Popondota)
Number of Christians: 3,281,502
        Roman Catholic (32%), Lutheran (16%), Uniting Church (10%)
Other faiths: Traditional beliefs (2.5%), Bahai (0.6%)

Parishes: 101
Number of clergy: 119
Theological colleges: Newton Theological College; Kerina Evangelist College

Brief history: The Anglican Church came to Papua New Guinea with the arrival of Fathers Albert Maclaren and Copeland King in 1891, near Dogura. In 1898 Papua New Guinea was organized as a missionary diocese of the Church in Australia. The first Papuan priest, Fr. Peter Rautamara, was ordained in 1914, and in 1960 the first indigenous bishop (George Ambo) was consecrated. The province was founded on February 27, 1977. It is governed by a Provincial Council and House of Bishops which meets once a year.

Archbishop: George S. Ambo
Provincial office: P.O. Box 304, Lae, M.P., Papua New Guinea
Provincial newspaper or magazine: *Family*

United Churches

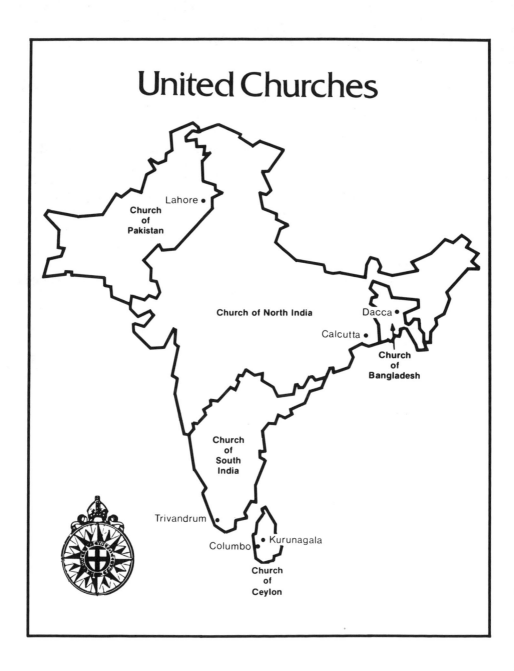

UNITED CHURCHES
Churches Formed by a Union of Anglicans with Christians of other Traditions

Church of South India

Geographical area: 1,269,346 square miles (all India)
Population: 746,742,000 (all India)
Number of members: 2,000,000
Dioceses: 21 (Coimbatore, Dornakal, East Kerala, Jaffina, Kanyakumari, Karim-
        nagar, Karnataka Central, Karnataka North, Karnataka South,
        Krishna-Godavari, Madhya Kerala, Madras, Madurai-Ramnad, Me-
        dak, Nandyal, North Kerala, Rayalseema, South Kerala, Tiruchirapalli-
        Thanjavur, Tirunelveli, Vellore)
Other Christian Churches: Roman Catholics (1.3%), Orthodox (0.2%)
Other faiths: Hindu (79%), Muslim (12%) (all India)

Number of congregations: 8,690
Number of clergy: 21 bishops and 1,267 presbyters (1984)

Brief history: The Church of South India is the oldest United Church and the
first to bring together Christians from Episcopal and non-Episcopal traditions.
After 20 years of negotiation, the new Church was inaugurated on 27 September 1947 and brought together Christians from the Anglican, Methodist, Presbyterian, Congregationalist and Reformed traditions.

Moderator: The Most Rev. I. Jesudasan, Bishop in South Kerala
Church headquarters: Synod Office, Cathedral P.O., Madras
Magazine: *The South India Churchman,* monthly

Church of North India

Countries: The Northern and Western parts of India and the Andamans and
Nicobar Islands
Number of members: 1,400,000
Dioceses: 23 (Agra, Amritsar, Andaman and Nicobar Islands, Assam, Barrack-
pore, Bhopal, Bombay, Calcutta, Chandigarh, Chotamagpur, Cuttack,
Darjeeling, Delhi, Durgapur, Gujarat, Jabalpur, Kolhapur, Lucknow,
Nagpur, Nasik, Patna, Rajasthan, Sambalpur)
Other Christian Churches: Roman Catholics (1.3%)
Other faiths: Hindu (79%), Muslim (12%)

Number of congregations: 2,000

Brief history: The Church of North India was inaugurated in 1970 and is a union
of six churches: The Anglican Church, the United Church of Northern India
(Congregationalist and Presbyterian), the Methodist Church (Brittish and Aus-
tralian Conferences), the Council of Baptist Churches in Northern India, the
Church of the Brethren in India, the Disciples of Christ. The Church of North
India shares the same early history as that of the Church of South India.

Presiding Bishop and Moderator: The Most Rev. Din Dayal, Bishop of Lucknow
Address of General Secretary: 16 Pandit Pant Marg, New Delhi 110001, India
Church magazine: *The North India Churchman,* monthly

The Church of Pakistan

Geographical area: 310,400 square miles
Population: 88,900,000
Number of members: 700,000
Dioceses: 8 (Faisalabad, Hydrabad, Karachi, Lahore, Multan, Peshawar, Rai-
      wind, Sialkot)
Other Christian Churches: Roman Catholics (0.5%)
Other faiths: Muslim (74%)

Number of congregations: 300
Theological colleges: Gujunurawala Seminary, Lahore; St. Thomas' Seminary,
      Karachi

Brief history: The Church of Pakistan was formed in 1970 as a Union between
four churches: The Church of Pakistan (Anglican), the United Church of North
India and Pakistan (Presbyterian), the United Methodist Church (American
Methodist), the Lutheran Church of Pakistan.

Moderator: J. S. Qadir Bakhsh
General Secretary: Dr. Vincent Das, Principal, Murray College, Sialkot, Pakistan

The Church of Bangladesh

Geographical area: 55,598 square miles
Population: 90,000,000
Number of Anglicans: 12,000
Dioceses: 1 (Dhaka)
Other Christian Churches: Roman Catholics (0.2%)
Other faiths: Muslim (86%), Hindu (13%)

Number of congregations: 55
Number of clergy: 20
Theological college: St. Andrew's Theological Training Centre, Dhaka (ecumenical).

Brief history: Bangladesh was previously East Pakistan. It was part of the State of Pakistan partitioned from India in 1947 to form a separate Muslim state. After a civil war between East and West Pakistan, which ended in 1971, East Pakistan became an independent state, Bangladesh. Before independence the Diocese of Dhaka was one of the dioceses of the Church of Pakistan and its early history is that of the Church of Pakistan. Today the Church has just one diocese and is a minority church in a minority religion.

Moderator: The Rt. Rev. Dwijen Mondal
Church headquarters: St. Thomas' Church, 54 Johnson Road, Dhaka 1, Bangladesh

Ecumenical and Inter-Church Relations

Churches in full communion with Anglican Churches

A majority of Anglican Provinces have ratified agreements of full communion with
1. The Church of South India
2. The Church of North India
3. The Church of Pakistan
4. The Church of Bangladesh
5. The Old Catholic Churches, Union of Utrecht
6. The Philippine Independent Church
7. The Mar Thoma Syrian Church of Malabar, India

The Old Catholic Churches of Europe and North America, with 443,000 members, were separated from the Roman Catholic Church at various times and for various reasons during the 18th and 19th centuries. They maintained the historic episcopate and many other elements of Catholic faith and order. In 1889 the Dutch, German and Swiss Old Catholic Churches united in a common profession of faith, the Declaration of Utrecht. The largest branch of the church, the Polish National Catholic Church, grew out of an ethnic dispute in the Roman Catholic Church in America in 1890.

The Bonn Agreement between Old Catholics and the Church of England in 1931 established full communion with the Church of England and was soon ratified by other Anglican Churches. Each national Church is governed by its own Synod of bishops, priests and laity. The Archbishop of Utrecht is Primate and Chairman of the International Old Catholic Bishops' Conference but only has jurisdictional power in his own diocese.

The Philippine Independent Church was established in 1902 by leaders of the popular revolution against Spain in 1896, which sought among other things religious emancipation and a national identity for Filipino Christians. Today it claims 4,000,000 members in 28 dioceses, with 50 bishops, 600 priests and 2,600 organized congregations. It sought and received consecration of its bishops in the apostolic succession from the Episcopal Church USA in 1961. Subsequently full communion was established with the Episcopal Church and other Anglican Provinces. Through a concordat it cooperates closely with the much smaller Philippine Episcopal Church and, since the 1950s, clergy of the two churches have been trained together at St. Andrew's Seminary in Manila.

The Mar Thoma Church traces its history through the Syrian Orthodox Church of Malabar, to the planting of Christianity in India by St. Thomas the Apostle.

In the 19th century a section of the Orthodox Church separated to form the Mar Thoma Church. This action was due partly to the influence of Anglican CMS missionaries working in India and relations between Mar Thoma Christians and Anglicans, or former Anglicans, in India have continued to be close. The Mar Thoma Church is now in full communion with the united churches of India and with most of the Anglican Communion. It includes an estimated 350,000 members in 5 dioceses and 640 congregations.

International Inter-Church Dialogues

1. The Anglican-Roman Catholic International Commission was established on the initiative of Pope Paul VI and the Archbishop of Canterbury and approved by the Lambeth Conference in 1968. The first commission published its *Final Report* in 1982, containing Agreed Statements on the Eucharist, Ministry and Authority in the Church. This was referred for study and response to all Anglican Provinces and to the various national conferences of Roman Catholic bishops. Meanwhile, a second international commission has been appointed and has issued its first report on *Salvation and the Church*.
Present co-chairmen: The Rt. Rev. Mark Santer, Bishop of Birmingham, Anglican; The Rt. Rev. Cormac Murphy-O'Connor, Bishop of Arundel and Brighton, Roman Catholic

2. Anglican-Lutheran Dialogues have developed mainly at the national or regional level, but with guidance and support from the Lutheran World Federation and the Anglican Consultative Council. In Europe discussions between representatives of the Church of England and the Scandinavian Lutheran Churches have continued regularly for over 50 years. In North America there have been two series of Lutheran-Episcopal Dialogues and a third series has begun. The first *international* dialogues, 1970-72, recommended (the Pullach Report) that conversations be continued, among the churches directly concerned, in Europe, the United States and Tanzania. Building upon the remarkable theological convergence achieved in the American conversations, the report of the Anglican-Lutheran European Commission 1980-83, *Anglican-Lutheran Dialogue,* agrees that the churches should establish full communion and discusses steps that need to be taken to achieve that goal.
Present co-chairmen: The Rt. Rev. David Tustin, Bishop of Grimsby, Anglican; the Rt. Rev. Sebastian Kolowa, Presiding Bishop, Evangelical Lutheran Church In Tanzania, Lutheran.

3. Anglican-Orthodox Joint Doctrinal Commission
Although Anglican-Orthodox relations have a history, through the Church of England, older than the Anglican Communion itself, the present series of official conversations began in 1973. Two Agreed Statements on basic theological matters have been published, the latest being the *Dublin Agreed Statements.*

Present co-chairmen: Professor John Ziziolas, Metropolitan of Pergamos; The Rt. Rev. Henry Hill, Anglican Church of Canada

4. The Anglican-Oriental Orthodox Forum held in Canterbury in 1985 brought together representatives of the Syrian, Armenian, Coptic and other Oriental churches, as "the beginning of a more systematic exchange" between Anglicans and those ancient churches. A second Forum is to be held in 1989 or 1990.

5. The Anglican-Reformed International Commission, 1978-83, was under the sponsorship of the ACC and the World Alliance of Reformed Churches. Their report, *God's Reign and Our Unity,* was published in 1984 and referred to the churches for study and response.
Co-Chairmen: The Rt. Rev. John Tinsley, then Bishop of Bristol, and the Rev. Roy F. Wilson, United Church of Canada.

Councils of Churches

The World Council of Churches includes in its membership nearly all member churches (Provinces) of the Anglican Communion. Eight were founding members of the WCC in 1948. It also provides a forum for ecumenical study and cooperation with a wide variety of churches, including those with whom we are in bi-lateral dialogues as described above. One result of such multilateral work over many years is the consensus statement issued by the WCC Faith and Order Commission under the title, *Baptism Eucharist and Ministry* (known also as *BEM,* or the *Lima Text).* Other aspects of the WCC program are summarized in the Lambeth Study Book, *The Emmaus Report,* p. 145ff.

Anglican Provinces are also active members of national and regional Councils of Churches in their own geographical areas.

For Further Reference

The World Christian Encyclopedia, David B. Barrett, ed.; 1982 Oxford University Press.

Anglican Information and **Anglican Media Mailing,** regular publications of the Anglican Consultative Council, 157 Waterloo Road, London SE1 8UT

Many Gifts, One Spirit, proceedings of ACC-7, Singapore 1987. Published for the ACC by Church House Publishing, London.

The Anglican Cycle of Prayer, published annually for ACC by Forward Movement Publications, Cincinnati. A daily prayer calendar including Anglican information and names of all dioceses and bishops in the Anglican Communion.

Highways and Hedges by Bishop John Howe, 1985, Anglican Book Centre, Toronto. The development of the Anglican Communion from 1958-1982 with emphasis on its ecumenical relations, by the first Secretary General of the ACC. Contains a helpful summary of the agenda of recent Lambeth Conferences and meetings of the Anglican Consultative Council.

Lambeth Study Books are available from Church House Publishing, London, Forward Movement Publications, Cincinnati, and other Anglican publishers. The list includes: **For the Sake of the Kingdom,** the report of the Inter-Anglican Theological and Doctrinal Commission; **Towards a Theology for Inter-Faith Dialogue; Open to the Spirit,** Anglicans and the experience of renewal, edited by Colin Craston; **Equal Partners,** popular report of the Mission Agencies Conference 1986, edited by Alan Nichols; **The Emmaus Report** on ecumenical relations, edited by Martin Reardon; **Salvation and the Church,** an Agreed Statement by ARCIC II; **God's Reign and Our Unity,** the report of the Anglican-Reformed International Commission; **Transforming Families and Communities,** the report of the International Project on Family and Community.

Information about individual Provinces may be obtained by writing to the Provincial Secretary whose address is given at the end of each Provincial Profile.